Dark Antonyms and Paradise

The Poetry of Rienzi Crusz

by

Chelva Kanaganayakam

TSAR
Toronto
1997

We acknowledge the support of the Canada Council for the Arts for our publishing program. We also acknowledge support from the Ontario Arts Council.

Cover art by Grant Donesky.

Canadian Cataloguing in Publication Data

Kanaganayakam, C. (Chelvanayakam), 1952–
Dark antonyms and paradise: the poetry of Rienzi Crusz

ISBN 0-920661-68-8

1. Crusz, Rienzi, 1925-
2. Poets, Canadian (English) - 20th century - Biography.* I. Title.

PS8555.R87Z72 1997 C811′.54 C97-931720-7
PR9199.3.C72Z72 1997

Printed in Canada by Coach House Printing.

TSAR Publications
P. O. Box 6996, Station A
Toronto, Ontario M5W 1X7

To my sister and brother, Sivam and Kumar

and to the memory of my sister Thilagam

ACKNOWLEDGEMENTS

Among the many people who made this study possible, the staff in the Doris Lewis Rare Book Room at the University of Waterloo Library deserve special mention: they made archival research a pleasure and I am grateful to them. I am also indebted to Rienzi Crusz who was always helpful and generous with his time; and to his wife Anne, for her translations of Sinhala words and for her traditional Sri Lankan hospitality. Nurjehan Aziz and M G Vassanji have been, as always, a source of immense support. At short notice, Uppinder Mehan and Linda Hutcheon agreed to read the manuscript, and their feedback was thorough and perceptive. I would like to proffer them my heartfelt thanks for their encouragement and sound advice.

The following abbreviations have been used
for the works by Rienzi Crusz:

FT *Flesh and Thorn*
EI *Elephant and Ice*
SW *Singing Against the Wind*
TL *A Time for Loving*
SR *Still Close to the Raven*
RD *The Rain Doesn't Know Me Any More*
BI *Beatitudes of Ice*

CONTENTS

1. Writing Against the Grain 1

2. Child of a Colonial Embrace 17

3. Paddy Fields and Snow Ploughs 30

4. A Death So Exotically Done 45

5. Visions, Confessions and Memoirs 62

6. Walking in the Penumbra 69

Notes 73

Selected Bibliography 79

Index 85

I want to see again what I have seen
to confirm former convictions and to know
that a certain vision is a continuing truth.

"The Oceans"— ZULFIKAR GHOSE[1]

I. WRITING AGAINST THE GRAIN

Striking a note of acceptance and resignation, Rienzi Crusz ends the last poem in his collection entitled *Still Close to the Raven* with the lines,

So, what's the essential story?
Nothing but a journey done,
a horizon that would never stand still.
(*SR* 75)

While the closure that the lines allude to is neither definitive nor consistent, the idea of a journey is never far from the poetry of Crusz. Time and again, the vision of "flights of birds," a "747 screaming," the "river's laughing face" and the contemplation of lands beyond the sea appear, reminding the reader of movement, of time, and a quest that remains unfulfilled. And for Crusz the journey is a complex one, involving, historically, the Portuguese arriving on the shores of Ceylon, politically, the realities of postcolonial Ceylon, and, autobiographically, his migration from Sri Lanka to Canada. To recognize one's place in these multiple journeys is also to acknowledge the ambivalence and flux of an identity that one would like to claim as unchanging and stable. Unwilling to espouse fixed positions, the poet speaks of conquest in terms that invoke romance and describes exile in images that recall paradise. And the constant movement from one pole to another, from praise to ironic denunciation, from acceptance to rejection, places him both within a whole body of postcolonial writing devoted to exile and at an angle to it.

Almost forty years ago, Alister Kershaw, the Australian writer, wrote a polemical and witty essay that criticizes the nostalgic yearning for home manifested among "fashionable" expatriate writers in

Europe—particularly those for whom the notion of home is fixed, monolithic, and historically constituted. With customary "slash and dash" Kershaw offers a spirited argument for retaining a "national" identity while living outside the geographical borders of the nation. Dismissing with characteristic cynicism the impulse to be "nuzzling once more at the benevolent teats of the mother country,"[2] Kershaw adds that "nationality"—the quirks and tics and prejudices and, no doubt, virtues which one picks up from one's early environment—must be pretty damned tenuous if it's endangered by going outside territorial waters."[3] Arguing that the impulse to valorize home in such terms amounts to a form of essentialism and repression, he ends on the note that "it's gloomily diverting to see so many of them yelping for their own final enslavement."[4] While not dismissive of origins and empathy with the land of one's birth, he advocates an internationalist stance that transcends narrow national allegiances and celebrates hybridity and cosmopolitanism—an attitude towards the idea of nations that anticipates the more contemporary views of cultural critics and authors such as James Clifford and Salman Rushdie.[5]

In response to this essay, Patrick White, who had after several years decided to make Australia his home, wrote a literary and autobiographical piece, appropriately called "The Prodigal Son," defending his decision to return to the land where "the march of material ugliness does not raise a quiver from the average nerves."[6] For White, the prospect of a philistine society is less forbidding, less daunting and destructive than a life of exile, condemned to remain a permanent outsider. Recalling the years he spent in Greece during and after World War II, "where perfection presents itself on every hand," he laments his feeling of alienation among the friendly Greeks and admits that "even the most genuine resident Hellenophile accepts automatically the vaguely comic role of Levantine beachcomer [sic]."[7] Hardly an abstract or essentialist concept, the notion of home, he claims, becomes a reality for one who embraces the landscape, becomes part of the quotidian world with all its imperfections.

White's resolution to return to Australia was a particularly fortunate one for him, for Castle Hill, (a suburb of Sydney), with all its limitations and pettiness, did transform him from a barely successful novelist and mediocre dramatist into the foremost writer of the country for more than two decades. The intensity—and often the exactitude—that characterizes his writing is of a kind made possible by a close involvement with the "bags and iron"[8] of the landscape. Here one sees a classic case of the "been to" becoming the voice and conscience of the country. And in White's assertion and in his fiction one sees the "nationalist" claims of postcolonial writing.

Kershaw's stance and scepticism about the centripetal force of the nation and stay-at-home attitude are probably equally valid, for if the nation is, as recent historiographic studies point out, in some ways an intellectual construct, then geographical distance must be less important than insight and perspective. According to this argument, living on the cusp between two worlds is a state of mind that leads to perception and empowerment not always accessible to those whose sense of affiliation is intertwined with borders and referential realities. Positioned on the margins, expatriate and diasporic writers see multiple worlds, palimpsests and consequently the contingency of monolithic claims. It is a view that Aamer Hussein characterizes as a doubling when he says about expatriation that "there is . . . a tremendous inherent privilege in the term, a mobility of mind if not always of matter, to which we as writers should lay claim: a doubling instead of a split."[9]

The space of exile as a particularly significant vantage point has been espoused by a number of contemporary writers and critics who see this niche as a privileged position—one that serves as a means of both escape and commitment. Writing and theorizing about the diasporic space has become increasingly common in an age of migrancy. Thus Salman Rushdie, for instance, writes about the experience of exile as refuge and as a crucible for new visions. As he puts it, "the broken glass is not merely a mirror of nostalgia. It is also, I believe, a useful tool with which to work in the present."[10] In a recent article, Vijay Mishra suggests the idea that the "diasporic space as the space of the border, a space that is always contaminated, now engenders the possibilities of exploring hybrid, cross-cultural and interdiasporic relationships."[11] It is a predicament that Gloria Anzaldúa analyzes imaginatively in *Borderlands* and claims that the new *mestiza* "learns to juggle cultures. She has a plural personality, she operates in a pluralistic mode—nothing is thrust out, the good the bad and the ugly, nothing rejected, nothing abandoned."[12]

While the notion of diasporic authors implies a common experience of displacement, for individual writers the actual uprooting has led to different forms of response. Mishra, for instance, theorizes about the various configurations of diaspora and offers a grid that paves the way for a taxonomy to accommodate a range of responses.[13] Along similar lines Aijaz Ahmad, in his discussion of Rushdie, draws attention to the principle of "excess" rather than loss as a condition and claim of migrancy.[14] Given the many personal, economic and political reasons that prompt exile, it is only natural for writers to choose from a whole spectrum of perspectives. For Roy Heath, the movement from the Caribbean to London has hardly altered his commitment to continue writing about his native Guyana. Having named Britain an alienating society— "a culture that has never been welcoming"[15]—he has steadfastly written about the Caribbean. A more immediate example of the relation between migrancy and nation might well be the work of Rohinton Mistry which consistently goes back to the land of his birth, and Canada, which has been his home for more than twenty years, has found no more than an occasional place in his writing. Such a reading has been sometimes contested and it has been suggested, not without validity, that Mistry is not exclusively Indian and that such labels, both unitary as in "Indian" and hyphenated as in "Indo-Canadian," are limiting and inaccurate. Granted, and yet there is a difference between the mindset that inspires the referentiality of *Such a Long Journey* and that which leads to the artifice of Michael Ondaatje's *The English Patient*. They suggest two very different responses to the diasporic predicament.

However, for most writers, including Rienzi Crusz, exile has entailed a duality involving both loss and gain, attachment and alienation. In a telling metaphor Abena Busia speaks about the predicament of being "stranded on the shores of saxon seas"[16] although she is aware that exile entails more than mere loss. Suniti Namjoshi describes the dispossession in equally ambivalent terms, in an image that establishes a difficult balance and opposition: "In the West I burn;/here,/when my lungs give out,/I cannot breathe."[17] Exile thus involves living between and with two worlds, placing one against the other, at once celebrating and subverting the two worlds. If this duality has accounted for a lot of the complexity associated with exilic writing, it has also been consistently problematic in that it often shifts the attention away from the writing to issues that are cultural and political.

The work of Rienzi Crusz is, willy nilly, embroiled in the ongoing concern with exile and belonging, for his sympathies seem to be as much with the rootedness of White as it is with the internationalism of Kershaw. He shares with Busia a longing for "home" while agreeing with Namjoshi that home can be stifling. However, identity is an issue which he also finds frustrating, particularly when arguments take on mutually exclusive positions, and criticism aligns itself with propaganda to "label" writers. At such times he would prefer to distance himself, for the formalist and perhaps the historian in him insist on synthesis which neither his critics (nor, for that matter, some of his own poetry) is willing to fully endorse. From his first collection entitled *Flesh and Thorn*, published in 1974, to his most recent volume *Beatitudes of Ice*, brought out in 1995, the most prominent issue for critics has been migrancy and the manner in which the author negotiates the two worlds of Sri Lanka and Canada.

Whether Crusz likes it or not, he has often been forced to assume a hyphenated identity, to wear the mantle of a multicultural writer. Formal and aesthetic concerns, notions of literary tradition and affinity with specific British, American and Spanish authors, for instance, have been deemphasized in order to focus on issues that seem more urgent, more relevant to the literary/cultural and political scene in Canada. The preoccupation with binaries and a concern with problems of alienation and exile have taken centre stage in most discussions.

If critics have at times tended to reinforce their own critical biases and positions in essays that are ostensibly about Crusz, the invitation to do so has come from the poetry itself. The titles *Flesh and Thorn*, *Elephant and Ice* and *Singing Against the Rain*, for example, all imply a binarism, as do several of the poems themselves. Apart from his first collection, all the binaries suggested by his subsequent volumes feed into ongoing concerns about the effects of colonialism and exile. Much more than White's preoccupation with Europe and Australia, the duality that Crusz deals with and invokes through his titles is politically charged and brings with it a variety of problematic issues —of history, colonialism, race, identity, and so forth. Neither indulging in nor retreating from this duality, Crusz inevitably—and inescapably —has become a writer whose corpus has nourished an ongoing debate about divided loyalties and about forms of essentialism, canonization, exoticism and ethnicity. Whether the themes of migrancy and identity are implied, as in "From Shovel to Self-Propelled Snowblower" (*SR* 16) or explicit as in "After the K-W Writer's award" (*BI* 65) the concerns refuse to be laid to rest, partly because the author never really frees himself from them and partly because the literary climate in Canada is hardly willing to jettison these concerns. As the author points out in his poem, "The Interview," the imaginary interviewer, whose solemnity, incidentally, is undercut by the poet's lack of attention, or rather, by the poet's concentration on something else, brings to the table a definite agenda and forces an acknowledgement of alienation:

> You coax me into beginnings,
> past inventions in the snow,
> then deftly persuade deeper fires,
> my thin Canadian ice
> to thaw in my throat,
> the maple leaf smudge in my passport.
> (*EI* 49)

The poet's own frustration seems to arise not from the subject matter itself but from an awareness of the naivete with which the polarities are established, with very little sense of the complexity, of how, for instance, "the elegiac and the ironic mix, with particular satiric potency."[18] The fluidity and contestatory quality of Crusz's work has often been ignored in formulations that are both topical and polemical.

Thus criticism on the poetry of Crusz has, from the beginning, focused on the two worlds of Sri Lanka and Canada that have been seen as the primary focus of his work. In a letter written in 1983, Crusz adopts a defensive posture when he says: "I'm not sure whether any serious writer would like to overemphasize the ethnicity of their writing, for like all good writers their concerns are universal, even though their idioms may be 'ethnic'."[19] Ironically, while the private correspondence with writers such as Travis Lane, Irving Layton and Zulfikar Ghose has often turned on issues of language, metaphor and the more formal aspects of his poetry, reviewers and critics—often conscious of the larger issues of cultural politics and the need to "place" the poet within a body of national or international literature—have been largely concerned with the implications of juxtaposing East and West. Much of the praise and a lot of the criticism came from those who felt exhilarated or jaded by the handling of these two worlds. Don Gutteridge, for instance, speaks about the two worlds in consistently laudatory terms. In a letter to the author he comments that "the Sri Lankan images juxtaposed to the quotidian Canadian are striking—and ultimately haunting."[20] More than two decades ago, in a letter written in 1973, Earle Birney comments: "you have already oriented or rather occidented yourself with the Canadian landscape and humanscape but without losing the rhythmic and emblematic traditions of Old Ceylon."[21] So does even Irving Layton in a telling metaphor about the two diametrically opposed worlds. Says Layton: "I especially like the way you spatter Ceylonese dung over the trim Canadian lawns."[22]

Writing about the two worlds, particularly in a context that is historically connected with forms of oppression and hegemony is at best a tightrope, and Crusz does in fact demonstrate how a bald thematization can be tiresome. Using the persona of his son, he writes:

Is he going mad
for the pot of honey,
forgetting the small pot-bellied child
he once was
in the green land of long ago?
It's the bubble, the bubble
he romps in, crazy
(*SR* 68)

And yet he does not—cannot—free himself from the pull of exile and its attendant dualisms. Among those unimpressed by the handling of the duality, Craig Tapping perhaps has been the most scathing in his attack of Crusz's work. In a review of Crusz's fourth volume of poems, namely, *A Time for Loving*, which appeared in an issue of *Canadian Literature*, he implicitly criticizes Reshard Gool, who writes the introduction to the book, and the poet for ignoring historical and social realities and creating a facile binarism that leads to deplorable forms of essentialism. "Sri Lanka is now subject to a colonial's dangerous nostalgia," claims Tapping, and goes to comment that "Crusz juxtaposes North American luxury with Sri Lankan underdevelopment, which is nonetheless privileged as more spiritually wholesome."[23] In his view, Crusz belongs to the same line of writers such as V S Naipaul who essentialise and distort the margins in order to find acceptance in the centre. Tapping does acknowledge the powerful imagism of Crusz's poetry, but the intent of his criticism is to demonstrate the link between the poetic and the political by showing how the poetry valorizes otherness through exotic evocations. The referential—the context of having to come to terms with two worlds —thus becomes the battleground for competing notions of idealism, nostalgia, essentialism, and bias of various kinds. Poetry gets enmeshed in the competing claims of labels, of "mainstream," "marginal," "multicultural," and so forth. Tapping places Crusz against a backdrop of postcolonial writing that celebrates recuperation and national identity and finds his work orientalist and at a remove from literature that validates itself as counter discourse.

In an essay titled "The Bourgeoisie That Fled the Revolution" Suwanda Sugunasiri takes Crusz and several other Sri Lankan poets writing in Canada to task for their antinationalistic stance and their failure to respond to and celebrate the revolution in Sri Lanka in the 1950s. As he sees it, their poetry has wilfully cut itself off from the sources of its inspiration and what is left are gestures of imitation. Sugunasiri positions himself very differently, in a manner that is sometimes problematic in that he employs a binary model to critique the binarism of Crusz. He and Tapping, however, arrive at similar conclusions about the role of the author's poetry. For Sugunasiri, Crusz belongs to a group of poets who, unwilling to participate in the Sinhalese cultural revivalism of the 1950s, left the country, and the act of desertion can only produce inauthentic verse, devoid of any real experiential depth and lacking in any commitment. According to Sugunasiri, while "Rienzi Crusz may not have hidden his immigrant status and seemingly identified with blackness . . . he is no closer to being Sinhalese or Sri Lankan than Ondaatje, in his sensibility or rootedness."[24] Here is yet another unitary and "nationalist" model being offered, and if one were to accept that as valid, then one should also admit that Crusz has spent much of his life writing against the grain.

Granted that writing which deals with issues of acceptance, assimilation, alienation and hybridity can hardly be neutral, the paradigm of opposition has had the effect of steering Crusz's poetry away from the pervasive irony, the self-conscious multiplicity, the contradictions and the formal concerns to a point where the extent to which the poet succeeds or fails as a multicultural writer with an acceptable political stance has become a primary concern. Crusz has clearly been unhappy with the ethnic grid that has been superimposed, sometimes with good intentions and very legitimate reasons, on his work and has tried, both in his self-reflexive poems and his occasional critical pieces to restore a sense of balance. In an important essay entitled "Talking for Myself" he says that "the elegies I wrote for my parents, the love poems for my wife, and the several poems I wrote on my children are important pieces in my repertoire. This was mainstream poetry if ever there was one; it counterbalances the separate and passionate elegies of the immigrant theme."[25] In fact, depending on the context, his readings have on occasion excluded all "ethnic" material, reinforcing that he could be both mainstream and marginal. Despite his pleas, and the candour with which he acknowledges rather than refutes the influence of a British tradition, labels of exclusion have persisted, at least partly because the literary (and political) climate in Canada is particularly conducive to such concerns.

It is true that some of the early reviewers and Crusz's critics have tended to go beyond or disregard ethnicity and respond to his poetry in formal terms, while not being unaware of the specificity of the imagery. A I Dust, for instance, speaks of the "wonderful controlled sexuality"[26] of the early poem "How Does One Reach the Sweet Kernel?" and Ghose, in a letter, refers to the "freshness of imagery" and the "fine feeling of sincerity behind the depiction of emotion."[27] Focusing on the ambivalence of the poet's treatment of love, W K Thomas, in a review of *Flesh and Thorn*, comments that "flesh . . . has its erotic delights, but sooner or later the thorn beneath the petal will be felt."[28] Very much along the same lines, Michael Thorpe, reviewing *The Rain*, claims that "Crusz continues to affirm in his poetry an undogmatic religion of life."[29]

It may well be argued that such claims that insist on the author's capacity for "powerful, universal poems" are as ideological as those that are overtly political and these attempts to transcend labels are a way of erasing otherness and imposing standards that are normative and mainstream. While the ideological underpinnings of ethnicity and formalism need to be dealt with in greater detail in subsequent chapters, suffice it to mention that Crusz's poetry often accommodates contrary pulls and thinks little of adopting a conciliatory or oppositional stance. Not unlike Derek Walcott, he uses all the traditions that are available to him, and if he moves from the poles of admiration and imitation to opposition and experiment, it is because the personal, historical and cultural circumstances make it necessary for him to do so.

Among diasporic writers the pull between memory and the immediate reality has often led to foregrounding one or the other. While the more dominant pattern has been as in the works of, say, Wilson Harris or Buchi Emecheta, to deal with the land that they left behind, or, alternatively, as with Thomas Keneally, to locate his fictions in lands other than Australia, Crusz has returned consistently to both worlds, for the simple reason that both worlds are crucial to his identity. In modes that are oppositional, complementary or ironic, the East and the West constantly surface in all his work. And his subjective position emerges in ways that are insistently ambivalent. Despite the pervasive pronominal "I" that attaches itself to the speaker of the poems, the manner in which the poet positions himself underscores the multiplicity of voices and attitudes. If ice is a metonym for the isolation and despondency of the poet in one poem, it mutates into an "igloo of heaven" in another. If "the beautiful slant/of raindrops" is the occasion for elegiac reminiscence, "bloated bodies / riding the dark currents to the sea" are a reminder of violence and ethnic strife in Sri Lanka. As Robert Crusz rightly observes, "Crusz's poetry is a creative example of the primary distinguishing mark of this 'fourth world' inhabitant, namely, having a cultural identity which is an ongoing process of *becoming*, never finally arriving."[30]

And this synthesis is closer to the notion of ambivalence (that critics such as Homi Bhabha have drawn attention to) than to simple opposition or slavish imitation. In Crusz there is little of the passionate rewritings of master narratives that is so characteristic of some postcolonial writing or the "anxiety of influence" (to use Harold Bloom's phrase and concept) to better the performance of canonical mainstream writers. Instead, there is a candid acceptance of the multiple traditions that necessitate a complex response rather than a straightforward agonistic one.

The two worlds which are his subject matter are constantly created and erased to make way for new configurations. Sri Lanka is the land of betrayal if one were to read the poems about his ex-wife as being partially allegorical or the more recent political poems as reflections and recent manifestations of his own predicament. And yet Sri Lanka is part of an elegiac yearning, the therapeutic impulse that drives his poems and leads to the creation of a pastoral world. These are both "real" and "imaginary" in that they are referential, but they are also constructed realities created by an ongoing quest for an identity acceptable to those who locate themselves on the cusp between worlds.

The refusal to participate in binaries appears again in the Canadian poems where the isolation is almost stifling and barbecues "burn like a small hell." McGiver becomes a personification of everything that is distancing in the country and hence becomes the target of all the irony and anger against an alienating environment. The poet's own complicity in such oppression also becomes the occasion for bitterness and self-contempt. But the new country is not entirely bleak; it is also a place of recuperation where the "vine hangs purple" and tortuous journeys end. To fail to see this layering in his work is also to miss his complex relation to the experience of migrancy.

This constant search is an aspect of the commitment to the problematic definition of identity. And the emotional momentum that the poetry picks up is always kept in check by the self-reflexivity and the irony that is "multi-directional" and fluid. The irony serves to mediate the experience of exile, to remind the reader that excessive centrism of any kind might well become an indulgence. About this ebb and flow and the function of irony as strategy, Hutcheon comments:

> For immigrants, the need to resist the dominant culture—however liberal or well-meaning—may be intensified because of the weight of cultural traditions, made heavier (not lighter) by distance and time, by memory, by a sense of exile or simple nostalgia. Therefore the drive towards self-definition within a new culture may well involve separation from ethnic past, at least temporarily. And irony is a useful device for articulating both the pull of that tradition and the need to contest it.[31]

This aspect, the reluctance to take totalizing positions, is a central aspect of Crusz's writing. But the collection that probably received the most attention, namely *Elephant and Ice*, works with dualities and this has led to the belief that his stance is fundamentally oppositional.

The political implications of such an approach can hardly be underestimated. Crusz and Michael Ondaatje, for instance, are both expatriates from Sri Lanka, both Burghers[32] who, after a brief period of stay in England, made Canada their home, and while Ondaatje has been consistently anthologised in Canadian poetry collections, Crusz has remained largely in his shadow, ghettoized under the multicultural label. While the relative merits of these two writers is not necessarily important, and while generalizations about who is the better poet can be futile, it is in fact true that Ondaatje has rarely been concerned (or associated) with East-West dichotomies, the only exception being *Running in the Family*. When asked about his response to the readers who would prefer him to write "Canadian" or "ethnic" novels, his response is unequivocal: "I feel little responsibility to that sort of demand."[33] While more recent criticism, particularly that which takes its cue from Arun Mukherjee's critique of Ondaatje's apolitical stance in the essay "The Poetry of Michael Ondaatje and Cyril Dabydeen"[34] has sought to address Ondaatje's conscious distancing from "ethnic" or multicultural issues, the author himself has successfully remained outside this classification. His conscious choice to explore landscapes other than Sri Lanka has been a factor in giving him the label "mainstream" unlike many other immigrant or exiled writers. Crusz, on the other hand, did in fact make ethnicity an integral part of his corpus. And he did pay a price for that involvement.

To be excluded from Canadian anthologies, for instance, is not simply a matter of recognition. It ties in with larger issues of canonicity, of the curriculum, with readership and reception. Acceptance and rejection are part of an interlocking system that establishes standards both nationally and internationally. And one who is denied a place is consequently denied a "national" status as a poet. And Crusz, then, is neither fully Sri Lankan nor Canadian and the limbo status has pushed him towards a measure of neglect among critics in Canada and in Sri Lanka. Rajiva Wijesinha's *An Anthology of Contemporary Sri Lankan Poetry in English* (1988), for instance, does not include selections from the poetry of Crusz, an omission that demonstrates the complexity of classification. And Arun Mukherjee points out that "Margaret Atwood's *The New Oxford Book of Canadian Verse in English* (1982) includes only two minority writers"[35] and the two are not particularly involved with ethnicity. Despite the fact that conditions have changed considerably since 1982, the general argument stills remains a valid one.

Critics such as Thorpe and Layton have had important things to say about Crusz. And Uma Parameswaran and Arun Mukherjee did in fact point to nuanced ways of reading the poet within a multicultural framework. Crusz himself found in this duality both a lover and a demon that he sought to embrace and exorcise. He sees the dualities, but, as subsequent chapters argue, he embraces forms of synthesis and the binaries lead to a holistic vision. Crusz provokes, challenges and destabilizes a narrow and schematic way of approaching the preoccupation with migration. His attempt has been to transcend the categories of nostalgia and essentialism to a new vision that embraces both worlds and moves beyond them. That he has often been frustrated is perhaps inevitable for reasons that Ranu Samantrai explains very clearly: "The concept of migrancy can be used for conservative as well as progressive ends. When, perhaps, despite itself, it reinforces the terms of home and belonging in order to authorize the migrant as the romantic exile/outsider, it plays into nationalist notions of the nation as an organic, homogeneous community."[36] Neither Crusz's personal history nor his literary training allows for the straightforward binary of centre and margin. He has claimed:

> The road forks
> like a wishbone:
> I choose neither, refuse
> the destinies in separate highways.
> And so I go for the crotch
> of no-man's land
> (*SR* 52)

Unfortunately, this remains an inadequately recognized part of his work.

In short, what has been inadequately recognized is that the metaphors of elephant and ice, or snow and raven are part of a larger poetic structure that accommodates a wide range of thematic concerns, including those of assimilation. His poetry has changed its emphasis over a period of time, has become passionate or restrained, explored the cerebral and exalted the subjective in his seven volumes of poetry. To see his contribution entails seeing him as more than a migrant or ethnic poet, not unaffected by the realities of Canada and Sri Lanka, but as one whose primary concern is with a passionate commitment to poetry itself.

Eschewing the modern and the postmodern, hardly concerned with what Joseph Conte has called the "serial" and "procedural"[37] forms of postmodern poetry, Crusz has been a writer of lyrics, very much in the Romantic tradition, concerned with the vicissitudes of personal life and the changing demands of heterogeneous cultural environment. Recuperative and therapeutic, his poetry is a personal statement—about his family, his children and about himself.

Thorpe makes a subtle and important point when he likens Crusz to the older generation of Commonwealth poets who could address the problematic issues of colonialism and migrancy without shrill denunciation. Paradoxical as it may seem, the distinction is an important one, for in the works of these writers the commitment is tempered by a consciousness of language, of emotion, of form. Having called Crusz "arguably the best living Sri Lankan poet in English" Thorpe adds that "though he has been in Canada since 1965, Crusz belongs to that older postcolonial generation, including such writers as Walcott and Soyinka, prepared to appropriate the legacy of Shakespeare and English without anguished breast-beating . . ."[38] At some level Derek Walcott is not only a Caribbean or St Lucian author but simply a poet; that is probably how Crusz needs to be seen.

Crusz as immigrant poet, as "ethnic" writer, has significant things to say. At a time when the claim of ethnicity is being seen not only as an integral part of the experiment of multiculturalism, but also as a corrective to so-called mainstream preoccupations, to see Crusz as the Sun-man or as the Raven is not without significance. But to foreground these to the point that the other aspects of his poetry are eclipsed would not only obscure the syncretic and multivocal aspect of his work but also ignore the more formal claims his poetry makes. Inherently complex and multiplicitous, his work is driven by impulses that are radically different from the tradition of modern and postmodern poetry. There is subversion and irony, but also a commitment to passion, a willingness to explore an inwardness while retaining an involvement with the referential, the social and the diasporic.

Crusz's early attempts to publish his poems were not always easy. Although he did succeed in having his poems brought out in *Canadian Forum, The Prairie Schooner, Fiddlehead, The Malahat Review,* and so forth, he recalls in conversation the impediments he faced, particularly with issues such as nostalgia, otherness and exoticism. Perhaps in all the battles for recognition and acceptance, what remained below the surface was the fact that at some level he was an outsider, not because he was ethnic, or that he spoke about the elephant and the raven, but because, while his intellectual makeup was shaped by a tradition that was British, North American and international, his subjectivity was moulded by a confluence of various other traditions. His poetry is an attempt to effect a marriage of opposites, to write against the grain, and this is where his achievement lies.

Crusz is, at some level, clearly an elegiac poet, constantly returning to his family, particularly his parents, who have been shaping influences in his life, giving to him that commitment to feeling and the obsession with precision in his work. The elegiac note which begins with the family extends beyond that to a somewhat idealized and "constructed" notion of the land, more important as tropes that signify a holistic life than as referential reality. It is this aspect that Tapping characterizes as nostalgia and essentialism rather than as metaphors to anchor an emotional attachment to the land.

This feeling of attachment, however, is tempered by a sharp sense of betrayal, by the woman he loved and the land he grew up in. The first he chooses to make the subject of a number of his early poems—ones that appeared in *Flesh and Thorn*—and the second he distances himself from, for reasons that are not difficult to imagine, although the occasional satirical poem is a reminder that politics is not entirely divorced from the poet's consciousness.

Spurned by Sri Lanka, the poet finds Canada a haven—a source of comfort that he celebrates in the children's story "Bumpis, the Magic Elephant."[39] Canada is also a country he understands at a visceral level, for his intellectual training, his hybrid lineage, his religious convictions are all Western. Hence the validity of Uma Parameswaran's comment that "landscape, not sensibility or educational background, is the difference between Crusz and native-born Canadians."[40] And yet everything in Canada is a constant reminder that he is an outsider, a "raven," a "sun-man."

If there is a part of him that resists the various closures that are demanded by the dominant culture, another part jettisons the whole project and retreats into a textual world, into the world of poetry. But the kind of poetry that appeals to him is neither contemporary nor "fashionable." Here again is an element that destabilizes the kind of affinity with postmodern forms of writing that, say, Ondaatje has established. Very much more in the tradition of Romanticism than modernism or postmodernism, he is still an anachronistic figure. If his capacity to work with symbols links him with the modernists, his insistence on authorial presence removes him from the modernist impulse. If the personal and the intimate aspects of his poetry make him contemporary, his consciousness of artifice alienates him from contemporary trends.

His difference is further compounded by his religious faith, a Catholicism whose love for the transcendental is mediated at times by an attitude of playfulness and irony that is as Hindu as it is Christian. How, then, does this faith coexist with a sharp consciousness of pain that runs through all his work? None of these is easily answered unless one were to adopt a teleological model for reading his poetry—a method that is likely to prove inadequate. It is possible to argue, on the basis of the titles he gives to his books, that the movement from "Flesh and Thorn" to "Beatitudes" is a linear one, although such a reading would be more convenient than accurate. As Robert Crusz observes, the desire is not for closure, not for a secure and enclosing frame, but rather "to give voice to the different constituencies of his identity which is always being formed."[41] It is hardly surprising that the river figures prominently as a trope in his poetry, for the image is a reminder that closure is inevitable but not necessarily an obsessive presence.

I had a sound colonial education
I have Dutch, nigger, and English in me,
and either I'm nobody, or I'm a nation

"The Schooner *Flight*"—Derek Walcott[1]

II. CHILD OF A COLONIAL EMBRACE

Immigrant literature, or literature of the diaspora, in its concern with the experience of two worlds, serves the useful function of destabilizing and subverting the assumption of homogeneity in the literature that shapes the canon of a nation. It defies the tacit understanding about norms of assimilation and negotiates alternative patterns of acceptance and acceptability. The same subversive potential of centre and margin, however, recapitulates yet another fallacy in that it assumes the two oppositional categories to be fixed and unalterable. It implies, in a Canadian context, the presence of a Canadian tradition and an "other" tradition that is shaped by the historical circumstance of colonisation and a common ideology of resistance. Particularly in the case of Crusz, such an assertion of duality is both inaccurate and problematic. If assimilation carries with it the suggestion of identification, and resistance the chasm of difference, for writers like Crusz, who are at home in both worlds, these categories can be confusing. Crusz cannot claim to be part of the centre; and he cannot, with any degree of sincerity, position himself as an "other." His allegiances remain contingent and indeterminate, and both his life and his work attest to that ambivalence.

Crusz began writing late; although his early life and his education were in some ways a preparation for his later poetry he was in fact well into his forties in Canada when the drudgery of working in the library at the University of Toronto, combined with other personal circumstances, triggered his writing. Thus there is very little by way of juvenilia to seek out in order to study patterns of evolution. A children's story called "Bumpis, the Magic Elephant," a prose work that is discussed in a later chapter, was written in the early sixties, but that was probably his only early attempt at writing. Apart from this, the only other "literary writing" was a piece that he wrote in his ex-wife's autograph book, a quotation from Shakespeare: "This above all/to thine own self be true,/ and as night follows the day/ Thou shalt be false to no man" which he includes in a recent poem entitled "Autograph Album."[2] He recalls in conversation the prophetic quality—and the irony—of having chosen those particular lines years before the breakup of his marriage.

What we do know, however, is the shaping of his sensibility, about which he speaks frankly in one of his rare personal essays and in his poetry. The essay reveals no anxiety, no self-consciousness or reticence about his thoroughly British education, a love for the Bible and for his interest in a long line of British and American poets. It is probably of some significance that the name "Rienzi" recalls the famous Roman orator and tribune and "Crusz" is clearly of Portuguese origin. It confirms the point that Uma Parameswaran makes when she says that "as a native-alien, Crusz's repertory has little of the treasures of classical or contemporary Tamil and Sinhalese literature that at least equal, and likely surpass, what Shakespeare, Milton or the Bible have to offer a South Asian Canadian writer. Crusz's literary heritage is first and last in the English language."[3] Ironically, it was his brother Hilary who, in addition to being a scientist, wrote poetry, while Rienzi was the recipient of a variety of influences, all of which were to shape his later writing.

The first and probably most important aspect of his background is the fact that he belonged to a very conservative Burgher family. The juxtaposition of "conservative" and "Burgher" is curious—even oxymoronic—particularly for those who have read Michael Ondaatje's *Running in the Family*, where the Burgher community is shown, for the most part, to be thoroughly hedonistic, bohemian and given to excesses of alcohol and tobacco. Such stereotypes were not altogether unknown in describing a community that included lawyers, doctors, civil servants, planters and sportsmen. Perhaps the fact that Crusz's family lived in Galle rather than in Colombo for a long time had something to do with Crusz's own upbringing, or maybe the fact that his father was first a teacher in Galle and then at St Peter's college in Colombo gave Crusz a very different perspective. His father Michael Crusz was first a teacher at St Aloysius College, Galle for 21 years and later at St Peter's College in Colombo. A mathematician, a disciplinarian and teetotaller, the father, trained by Jesuits and influenced by them, was a decisive influence in the family that consisted of seven sons and a daughter. As Rienzi's brother Noel wrote in an eulogy on the death of their brother Hilary, the father "was for all of us the ONE model."[4] In his essay, he talks about his father's extensive library, his love for mathematics and his familiarity with English poetry from an early age. The "elegy" that appears at the end of *Flesh and Thorn* is a remarkable poem, written with restraint, about a man who was deeply loved by the family. As he puts it:

You deserve a poem
exact as the sun,
with no beginning, no end,
just an intense line of light
curving to pure circle
(*FT* n.p.)

If the scientific frame of mind—"the cold arches of the brain" as he puts it in another poem" was acquired from his father, the artistic impulse came from his less-educated mother who, nonetheless, belonged to a family of architects and sculptors. In yet another poem entitled "Elegy" the poet recalls:

and how you loved the rose—
with cowdung, bonemeal and crushed eggshells;
the pomegranate tree
always so heavy with promise,
the shoeflower hedge pruned
to a prayer.
(*TL* 80)

About his parents, Crusz writes in a letter: "My father was the intellectual, the Renaissance man, the gentle liberal—my mother was the one who really kept us in shape in all ways—a tough but loving lady."[5]

Although not a prolific poet, his brother Hilary—who later became a distinguished professor of Zoology at the University of Peradeniya—was a lover of poetry, and Crusz speaks of *listening* to his brother's reading of Francis Thompson's "Hound of Heaven" and imbibing something of its rhythmic resonance. The oral quality that strikes the reader so insistently in Crusz's poetry is at least in part a result of this early influence in his life of listening to the brother, the Bible, the Psalms and Shakespeare in the film versions of *Romeo and Juliet* and *Julius Caesar*. His brother was a lay apostle, in addition to being a scientist, and that again is cocnsistent with the strong Catholic background of the family. His love for his brother and his love of religion are both evident in the poem "Elegy for an Elder Brother" (*RD* 66) which was written soon after his brother's death.

In the eulogy entitled "A Don's Journey to Science and God," Noel Crusz speaks of the early years of "beachcombing in the ancestral home in Kaluwella, Galle,"[6] a background that acquires a particular resonance in Crusz's poetry. The period in Galle was a brief one and the family moved to Colombo in the late 1920s (a few years after Rienzi was born in 1925) where he remained—apart from a two-year period in England—until he left for Canada. About Hilary Crusz, there is in fact more information, largely through the documentary film entitled *In Between* made by his son Robert for the BBC.[7] A powerful film about the dispossession of the Burghers, *In Between* is also an important source for understanding the world of Rienzi Crusz which, even to those who grew up in Sri Lanka, would seem unusual. English speaking, middle class, Catholic, the Burgher world absorbed and depicted the best of East and West. It reflected a truly multicultural Sri Lanka, where reading Milton and listening to a Sinhala love song were natural and even cherished. The film, with its insistent quest motif, its self-conscious deemphasis of the various political upheavals of the 1970s and 1980s, provides a useful backdrop for the study of Rienzi Crusz.

Crusz's education, again, suggests very little of a poet in the making, apart from a family that loved literature. After his high school education at St Joseph's and St Peter's Colleges in Colombo, he then received his university education in the University of Colombo. He recalls in his essay his disappointment when he was asked to read I A Richards's *Principles of Literary Criticism* before reading T S Eliot at the university, a suggestion not altogether surprising given the particularly Leavisite orientation of English studies in Sri Lanka at that time, and his decision to pursue history instead of English. "As for English literature," says Crusz, "I came to it on my own terms, in my own time. The switch was beneficial. I was not saddled with the burden of critical theory; I could do the free and separate thing. I could create my own idiom and mythology."[8] As for reading history, he refers to it with irony and amusement:

I didn't make it at university.
came out with only
some minute scars
of Buddhist Civilization
and Ancient History
gnawing in my brain.
(*FT* n.p.)

After graduating in 1948, the next three years he worked as a lecturer in history at St Joseph's College in Colombo. Switching disciplines again, this time into library science, he left for England in 1951 on a Colombo Plan Scholarship to the Morley School of Librarianship and Archives at the University of London. Upon his return he became the Chief Research Librarian at the Central Bank of Ceylon, a position he held until the more pressing personal circumstances and the growing nationalism in public life pushed him towards migration. During this time it was largely his reading of the poets—Shakespeare, Milton, Donne—and perhaps his familiarity with Neruda (who was, for a period of time, the Chilean ambassador in Ceylon) that shaped his consciousness.

Crusz's year of graduation was also the year of national independence. The next ten years were a period of sweeping changes intended to decolonize the country, among which the most symbolic was the jettisoning of English as the medium of instruction and the official language of the country. Crusz rarely discusses the politics of the time in Sri Lanka or the influence of the political situation in the country. His political poems are anecdotal, satiric, and constitute a relatively insignificant part of his overall writing. Poems such as "Dark Antonyms in Paradise" (*SR* 39) and "In the Shadow of the Tiger" (*SR* 30) belong to a much later period when social inequalities were becoming increasingly apparent and Tamil militancy was beginning to change the nature of ethnic conflict in the country. The 1960s were, however, a period of increasing nationalism—a process that became evident in the ethnic riots of 1958—in the country and the official language act was the first major political decision that alienated the Burghers and accelerated their departure from the country.

Crusz himself recalls the moment when one of the clerks at the Central Bank deliberately gave him a copy of the minutes written in Sinhala, a reminder that English was soon to be a thing of the past, and those who could function only with English were equally irrelevant in the new political climate.

The Burghers, whose first (and sometimes the only) language was English, were now seen for the most part as the legacy of the British and were targets for discrimination. The political climate brought to the fore what Ondaatje discusses in *Running in the Family* where he mentions that in response to a question from the Governor about identity, Emil Daniels had replied "God alone knows, your excellency."[9] Crusz himself draws attention to this in "Roots" which not unlike "Bouquet" in a later collection, about which Travis Lane points out in a letter, that it must have been a "difficult poem to write"[10] partly because of the popularity of the theme among postcolonial writers, but also because one would assume it amounts to admitting a particularly ambiguous status in the country of one's birth. To proclaim one's hybridity is problematic in a poem about "roots" and the poet confesses:

> I conjure history from a cup
> of warm Portuguese blood
> from my forefathers,
> black diamond eyes, charcoal hair
> from my Sinhalese mothers
> (*SW* 42)

In poems such as this and more so in "Bouquet" one is reminded of Walcott, for he too claims a mixed ancestry, one that problematizes the issue of identity.

This is what it meant to be a Burgher in Sri Lanka, a relic of a past that the country must disown in its zeal and haste to shed its colonial baggage. Of the writers who remained in the country after the changes in the 1960s, an important voice is Jean Arasanayagam, a Burgher married to a Tamil. She speaks of the loss of identity along very much the same lines in a poem entitled "Exile" where she wonders "what do I call myself/ Exile, emigre, refugee."[11] What was a matter of government policy was also reflected in day-to-day affairs, and Crusz sensed the increasingly difficult predicament of functioning in a postcolonial nation where one is thought of in some ways as being pseudowhite. While his brother, Hilary, for instance, chose to remain, the younger brother decided to emigrate.

While the political pressures were gradual and less noticeable, the more immediate circumstance that precipitated the departure from the country was the breakdown of his marriage when his wife left him. Naturally, Crusz has not been forthcoming about this period, but it was a time of immense pain, a sense of loss and betrayal and a redoubled responsibility of caring for the three children. If one were to look at the range of his poetry, and the paradox of immense pain and an equally strong faith, one needs to understand this phase of disillusionment which began with his departure for England and culminated soon after his return. Crusz himself says that "the first poems I wrote were written in the classic contexts of pain and memory,"[12] and he adds that the "'broken marriage, the sad exodus from Ceylon with three small children, provided excellent material to 'bring some order out of chaos'."[13]

To read many of the poems in *Flesh and Thorn* is to grasp the raw pain, the trauma caused by the breakdown of his marriage. As he puts it in lines strongly reminiscent of Dylan Thomas,

Then cats wailed
on the parapet wall,
and the wind called,
called through the na trees,
and she rose like a zombie
and walked into her beloved night.
(*FT* n.p.)

Drawing attention to the poem entitled "Biography," Parameswaran maintains that "the history of a broken marriage is succinctly conveyed—her refusal to be held in the persona's arms, her secret trysts elsewhere, and the intense hold on him even long after she disappeared into the night."[14] The relation between this pain and the therapeutic value of his poetry becomes the subject of the poem "The Roses Are the Color of Blood":

She opened a vein
and planted a rose,

the thorns she kept
for herself.

In the embrace of the wound,
from bruising and bleeding,

poet and muse
make poetry.
(*SW* 64)

The abandonment was such that he could not remain in the country. The personal, by a strange twist of fate, echoed the political, thus making the departure inevitable. And yet the country has remained very much a part of his identity, and the memories continue to be a source of much of his later poetry. The poems that have been sometimes called "nostalgic" and "exotic" are part of the pull of the land—ancestral memory for want of a better term—that draws him back. His periodic trips to Sri Lanka have been consistent, never a permanent move, but inevitable nonetheless. In 1981, a period of study leave from the library at the University of Waterloo (to which he had moved after a brief stint at the University of Toronto), where he worked as a Reference Librarian from 1969 to 1994, was the occasion to complete his children's story "Bumpis, the Magic Elephant." It was also the occasion to visit Kadugannawa, the home of the folkhero and Robin Hood figure, Sardiel, whose life and activities become the subject of several poems and a long prose piece that is yet to be published. His nostalgia—if one could use such a loaded term in a positive sense—is shaped by something more primal: the same impulse that draws Ondaatje to the landscapes of Sri Lanka in *Running in the Family*. In a recent unpublished poem, Crusz reiterates this commitment by telling his present wife:

tell the raven and the elephant
that I still sing their extravagant song,
parade their metaphors
without compromise.[15]

Neither the background nor the circumstances of his departure allows for a straightforward reading of the situation of exile. If his impulse to write was spurred by personal and political reasons, the intellectual baggage he came with and the climate of literary activity he found himself in necessitated an apolitical and even conservative stance at the beginning. The movement from Toronto to Waterloo, the stability of a regular income, the second marriage to a woman about whom he writes with deep affection, the children growing up, all these contributed to the movement from the private to the public sphere, to the range of themes that runs through his poetry.

His initial writing in the late 1960s was an attempt to exorcise his private demons, to give expression to a range of emotions, to come to terms with living in an alien land. Although the boredom of having to "produce five hundred edited cards" in the library at the University of Toronto was the immediate catalyst for his poetry, the subject matter involved an alien land and intense emotion, neither of which is seen as acceptable in the literary climate of the day. His first attempts to publish his poems in Canada were not always successful, although three of his poems—"The Accepted One," "Return of the Fisherman" and "Yesterday and Today"—were published by *Liontayles* in 1968. The same year he also published in *The American Poet, Cardinal Poetry Quarterly, United Poets* and *Voices International*. He recalls that his early poems found publication in *The New York Quarterly* and the *Prairie Schooner*, both American journals. Canadian journals soon recognized his merits despite the differences in subject matter, and between 1969 and 1972 the journals he was published in included *Quarry, Malahat Review, Canadian Forum, Fiddlehead, Prism International*, and several others. It was also a time when he faced some opposition because of his subject matter and his poetics that favoured the poetry of sensibility. He mentions in conversation how "Remains of an Oriental Poet" was written soon after a rejection of some poems from *Canadian Forum* on the grounds that they were too exotic. This poem was a response to that allegation and he wrote a carefully structured, tonally perfect poem that was minimalist and restrained. And given his tradition, it is hardly surprising that echoes of Milton, Hopkins, and Eliot (as in the lines "I have measured my pain/ on two continents:/ a pulsing thermometer dug/ into the mouth of the sun" *FT*, n.p) are prominent. Starting in 1971, *The Chevron*, the student newspaper produced at the University of Waterloo, has consistently printed and highlighted his poetry, thereby making his poetry popular among the academic community in Waterloo. It was also a high point in his recognition in the Canadian literary scene when *Descant* published eight of his poems in one issue in 83/84. More significant perhaps was the prize given to him for his religious poetry (specifically, "The Accepted One") and later the

Kitchener-Waterloo award for his poetry, about which he wrote an amusing and thoughtful poem. Although his poems have now been included in more than eighteen anthologies, the recognition was a long and difficult process, caused no doubt partly by his thematic preoccupations and partly by the literary climate in Canada.

Less impressed by the restraint of Imagism and the abstractions of Symbolism, he appears to have favoured the mode of the Romantic poets and that of Walt Whitman, Dylan Thomas and Pablo Neruda, who during his stay as Chilean ambassador in Sri Lanka lived not far from where Crusz grew up, and the rich ambivalence of Derek Walcott. On the one hand there is in him a strong adherence to traditional British literature. As he puts it, "if one has chosen to write in Shakespeare's tongue, then one must live or die by its idioms and rules."[16] And yet he appears to have been less impressed by the Eliot and Pound tradition of objective, minimalist writing. To quote Crusz: "Yes, I have heard of the 'spare line,' all about adjectival dross, Eliot's 'objective correlative,' . . . but what was, and is, most important to me is the 'song'."[17] Herein lie the peculiar paradoxes that surround his work.

Derek Walcott appears as an intertextual reference in his later poetry, and it is hardly surprising that he found in Walcott a definite affinity. One is reminded of the strong classical background similar to Walcott's, and the ambivalence of which Walcott speaks in relation to his own ancestry. The epigraph from Walcott itself suggests a nationalist and recuperative ambition in Walcott which is never fully realized in Crusz, at least not in the mode of the St Lucian poet:

> upon your penitential morning,
> some skull must rub its memory with ashes,
> some mind must squat down howling in your dust,
> some hand must crawl and recollect your rubbish
> someone must write your poems.[18]

Walcott's project is more "national" in that it attempts to write the history of the Caribbean and its people. Crusz, on the other hand, gives expression to remembered realities that are more personal than national.

Crusz's resistance to more readily available categories suggest a formalism and a conservative impulse which is not really true. In fact Arun Mukherjee argues for the opposite in several articles where she compares Michael Ondaatje and Crusz and shows the difference in their approaches. The comparison is a very useful one and has been used more often in critical studies dealing with Ondaatje than in the treatment of Crusz. Where Ondaatje is seen in some ways as turning his back on the country of his birth, in Crusz Mukherjee sees a commitment to the land. Where the former's stance is assimilationist, the latter's is more oppositional.

While such distinctions are in fact important differences, one needs to be aware that these attitudes are parts of a more complex whole. Crusz began by publishing *Flesh and Thorn* with Pasdeloup Press, a project encouraged by Virgil Burnett, who also drew the illustrations for this remarkable edition, and the next two with Porcupine's Quill. During this phase he found encouragement in the comments of poets such as Irving Layton, Harold Harwood, Travis Lane, Earle Birney and Robert Bly. In later years, in the early 1980s, the newly founded *TSAR* (Toronto South Asian Review) began publishing his work and has brought out four collections. He also found in Reshard Gool, Michael Thorpe, Zulfikar Ghose, Arun Mukherjee and Uma Parameswaran among others, friends, admirers and editors. His association with the *Toronto South Asian Review* publishers would suggest a political stance, a positioning on the margins which is partially true. The immigrant encounter, the oppositional stance, are germane to his writing, but to stress them at the expense of all others is to falsify his range.

Tapping, in his review, found in Crusz a suppressed Imagist. Travis Lane in her letters finds in the animal poems a relation to Marianne Moore.[19] Perhaps it is equally possible to see in his thematic concerns connections with a number of postcolonial poets. These comparisons are not about the anxiety of influence. Rather they caution the reader against an overanxious need to offer a taxonomy for a poet who occupies a complex space. Crusz himself seems to find this need to align himself with one group or another tiresome and counterproductive. He ends the most recent collection, *Beatitudes of Ice*, with a catalogue of all the poets, Eastern and Western, who have in various ways been mentors, shown him how to "dance in the rarefied air."

And yet, in relation to his compatriot Michael Ondaatje, Crusz remains a relatively marginalized poet whose work has not received the recognition it deserves. Literary histories hardly ever mention him and he remains marginalised in Canada and in Sri Lanka. Surveys assume patterns in order to establish a typology and Crusz's work with its curious admixture of traditional British forms and Sri Lankan images proves to be something of an anomaly. David Solway, writing in 1985, claims that "the classical idea of poetry as requiring elevated diction—as commanding a unique language distinct from both prose and ordinary speech, equipped with a peculiar set of rules, conventions, and formal exclusions—is now considered as an exercise in brahmanic arrogance and anachronistic fatuity."[20] If Crusz does not entirely fall into this category he is close enough in that he eschews the experimental in favour of the lyrical and the traditional. What constitutes the canon, how it is formed and how it is sustained are all problematic. As Robert Lecker rightly points out, "there is still no sustained consideration of how a (shifting) Canadian canon—if such an animal exists—can be seen as historically contingent, politically self-serving, ideologically generated and culture-ridden."[21] But it is clear that the last three decades have witnessed the creation of a canon and a counter-canon, the latter explained by the fact that writers such as Rohinton Mistry and M G Vassanji, for instance, have done extremely well in Canada. The emergence of literary magazines like the *Toronto South Asian Review* (1981), now the *Toronto Review of Contemporary Writing Abroad, Asianadian* (now defunct), *Watno Dur* (now defunct), *Ankur, Serai* and *Rungh*, and small presses like Williams-Wallace (now defunct), Vesta, Sister Vision and TSAR, is yet another example of the way in which a counter canon is gradually formed, a process aided no doubt by the growing interest in postcolonial studies in all the major universities in Canada.

Both within the canon and the counter-canon, Crusz has remained an outsider. Aijaz Ahmad points out that "the axiomatic fact about *any* canon formation, even when it initially takes shape as a counter-canon, is that when a period is defined and homogenized, or the desired literary typology is constructed, the canonizing agency selects certain kinds of authors, texts, styles . . . privileging them over others . . ."[22] In that process the ideological ambivalence of Crusz, an inevitable result of both personal and cultural circumstances, has for the most part worked against him. The binarism that creates the canon and counter canon leaves behind those that fall in the middle. In the editorial to an issue of *Canadian Literature* devoted to South

Asian writing, W H New makes the reminder that "European vicissitudes are not the only influences that have been shaping Canada"[23] and warns that "the cast of mind that defines by claiming universal truths—and then sustains these 'truths' by excluding 'messy' alternatives—appears to enjoy the neatness of categories . . ."[24] And yet categories have been difficult to avoid, and among the casualties of such a typology, Crusz is one. Canadian literature is a formidable institution that serves a normative function locally and in countries where it is taught in a systematic manner. Some texts and anthologies have shown an awareness of the effects of such a process. Kudchetkar and Begum introduce their anthology *Canadian Voices* by claiming that "the concept of Canadianness has itself to be problematized."[25] It is in such a space that Crusz locates his work.

In a literary culture that is attempting to define the notion of a Canadian classic and sifting and consolidating the various trends of the previous decades, writers such as Crusz are difficult to classify or accommodate. The features that define his work, particularly his lyricism, his emphasis on feeling and subjectivity, his nostalgia and distrust of the land he left, his ambivalence towards Canada, his love for the classics and his reliance on the landscape of Sri Lanka for his metaphors, these place him outside the canon. In attitude if not in ontology, his work is not unlike Walcott's *Omeros*—an unabashed celebration of a western tradition while being aware of the influence of a complex historical legacy.

Not I, some child, born in a marvellous year,
Will learn the trick of standing upright here.

"The Skeleton of the Great Moa in the Canterbury Museum, Christchurch"—ALLEN CURNOW[1]

III. PADDY FIELDS AND SNOW PLOUGHS

Among the seven volumes and several hundred poems that have been published in the last twenty-five years, the majority of the thirty-eight new poems in *Elephant and Ice* (1980) lend themselves most readily to the notion of "immigrant poet" that has defined and framed Crusz's work. Arun Mukherjee's valuable article that appeared in 1987, for instance, bears the title "Songs of an Immigrant," and she maintains that Crusz reveals in his work "what it is to be an immigrant and a non-white in a society that is so dissimilar from that of one's origin."[2] Along the same lines Kudchetkar and Jameela Begum maintain that writers like him "seek to establish an identity rooted in their traditional values and culture through a language that is indigenous and vernacular . . . "[3] Subsequent volumes have traversed new ground and worked with different perspectives, but the immigrant theme has remained a constant preoccupation. If anything, a title such as *Singing Against the Rain* suggests the need to increase the voice of opposition rather than sing in muted terms. However, if there is one label that Crusz probably has mixed feelings about, it is that of the "ethnic" or "immigrant" poet, despite the fact that the label came into being for perfectly legitimate reasons, and it was one that he unconsciously courted by writing a certain kind of poem. What is one part—albeit a constitutive one—of a total corpus has become, much to his dis-ease, the signature of his poetry. And *Elephant and Ice* has served as the metonym for his oeuvre, although he has gone on to explore a much more complex spectrum of ideas in his poetry. In addition to the implied binary of the title, the two images of elephant and ice reinforce the theme of identity politics which critics have often focused on to discuss his poetry. Subsequent titles, though less schematic, do draw attention to an oppositional stance and flaunt an otherness more forcefully than even some other poets whose preoccupation is more overtly and consistently about the politics of otherness.

As early as with the publication of *Flesh and Thorn* in 1974, the notion of assimilation and resistance began to be felt as integral to the poet's vision. Since Crusz had come to Canada only nine years earlier, such a stance seems hardly surprising. In a letter dated 18 June 1974, his brother Hilary writes about the need to move beyond cultural conflict. "My hope" says Hilary Crusz, "is that you will now use all this feeling and power to turn to hundreds of other subjects so that you will ultimately turn out to be a poet of vaster vision that will make for universality."[4] Even Irving Layton who has consistently praised the passion that underlies Crusz's poetry writes in a letter dated 6 March 1969 that "your further development will probably be marked by a greater care for the formal elements that go into the making of a poem . . . "[5]

Not surprisingly, reviewers of the first book seem similarly inclined to stress the unfamiliar and recognize that the familiar appears strange to this migrant poet. More than one critic has drawn attention to the quality of his perception which transforms what is banal to a "Canadian" into something striking as in "knives under your shoes" in "Little Brown Boy." According to Peter Stevens, the former editor of *Canadian Forum*, "the language of the poetry shuttles easily between the exotic references to such things as the jambu and the cadju-pulang trees and straightforward North American scenes."[6] Don McKay, the Canadian poet who was for several years editor of *Fiddlehead*, comments along the same lines but is wary about the implications of a binary stance. According to him, "Rienzi Crusz's book . . . is, in the context of Canadian poetry, exotic. It is unfortunate that a word like that can become the closet in the basement which keeps the parlour, furnished in plain pine replicas, tidy."[7]

For Stevens, McKay, and several others, the term "exotic" suggests itself quite naturally in the face of a constellation of imagery whose sources are totally alien to Canadian soil. With stanzas such as

> How at dawn,
> he would sit in the sun,
> with the mynah bird

breakfasting on the lawn,
listen to the raven chanting
to itself, the tall paddies
murmuring in the wind.
(*EI* 20)

establishing quite deliberately the distinction between the two worlds, the critical vocabulary naturally forms itself around binary terms. Crusz probably did intend these to be markers that evoked certain experiences, although not along the lines of exoticism. His comments in his essay that "some critics . . . have fallen into the trap of perceiving my own images . . . as mostly a visual and exotic exercise,"[8] is as much a reflection of his frustration as it is of the problematic relation between intention and reception. For a poet to be concerned, solely, with the "visual and exotic" then, is to write a kind of travelogue, the kind that falsifies emotion and becomes a mimicry of a colonising impulse. On the other hand, to draw quite naturally from this fund of images is also a gesture of resistance and a mark of authenticity. In fact, Mukherjee is right in asserting that Crusz has "created his own mythology and rhetoric because the available conventions of Anglo-Canadian poetry do not serve his needs."[9]

At one level, Crusz appears to have been concerned about flaunting the immigrant theme, and the self-reflexive irony about such indulgence makes itself felt in several of his poems. He wonders,

And what's so new
about this immigrant theme
that tattoos his work like a woodpecker?
The Red Man is right.
Everybody else is an immigrant.
(*SW* 68)

In his poetry, as in his critical piece, there is a cautiousness, a hesitancy and an awareness about working with dualities, although he also recognizes the inevitability of these concerns. In "The Interview" he realises that, when he is persuaded to talk about his beginnings,

I find my own, green forest, island sea:
the ocelot's eye, the jambu bleeds,

my childhood dreams
in the claws of sand crab.
(*EI* 49)

In short, in the process of writing about a land unfamiliar to Canadian readers and in defamiliarizing what Canadian readers take for granted, Crusz establishes a niche that is both distinctive and limiting. It calls into being the notion of ethnicity, which like so many other similar terms can be both neutral and politically loaded, depending on the circumstances. As Graham Huggan rightly maintains, "ethnicity, for a dominant culture, may be just another codeword for the foreign. This view of ethnicity sanctions ignorance while proclaiming the virtue of cultural tolerance. The ethnic label denotes cultural otherness without attempting to account for it."[10] In this somewhat extreme context that does not include Canadians who define themselves multiculturally, ethnicity becomes a formula for polite exclusion from Anglo-Canadianness.

To be ethnic in this scenario means to be somehow only marginally Canadian. When the author is seen to be not Canadian and at best hyphenated and when his or her writing recalls and recreates a world that is not Canada, then the status of the work as Canadian writing becomes suspect. This remains a problematic issue and has been dealt with in various ways by, among others, Arnold Itwaru in *Closed Entrances*, Neil Bissoondath in *Selling Illusions*,[11] and so forth. Regardless of how this argument is configured, the position of Crusz remains at an angle to this debate, not fully a part of it but not totally divorced from it either.

Arun Mukherjee, in several of her essays that deal with South Asian writing, attempts to dispel many of the myths that accompany ethnicity in the work of Ondaatje, Dabydeen, Crusz and others. Her project is to show, among other things, the inadequacy and ideological assumptions of Ondaatje's universalist stance and praise the commitment of poets such as Crusz. In her essay on Crusz's poetry, she points out that "like so many other third world Calibans who must perforce speak Prospero's tongue, Crusz wrestles with its inadequacies in order to communicate with the world from the vantage point of his otherness."[12] Mukherjee's review is a case in point where she attempts to celebrate the duality of East and West, to speak of it in cultural and political terms. Her stance is an important one, and a perfectly reasonable one, but it has had the effect of framing and foregrounding Crusz's work along mainly political lines.

Mukherjee is cautious in her praise and she makes it evident that the dividing line between authenticity and essentialism is often problematic. She maintains that Crusz "does occasionally become clumsily nostalgic and also indulges in exoticism."[13] While she is critical of such "word-painting" she also sees the need to move away from the comfortable niche established by "native born" Canadians. And she finds the irony and understatement in Crusz to be a lot more effective than mere hysterical outpouring and overtly tendentious writing. Despite the care with which she frames her analysis, her general argument appears to favour the foregrounding of what is "native" above the imitative.

According to this line of thinking, to deny one's ethnicity is a form of hypocrisy that allows for assimilation under the banner of Eurocentric universalism, whereas to advertise one's ethnicity is to establish one's claim on one's own terms. As Huggan puts it in a different context, "to write ethnicity is to advertise one's perceived ambivalence: it is, in part, to consider oneself as other . . . "[14] While some of Crusz's poems do belong to this category, others don't.

At its most obvious, the personae he adopts—the Sun-man and less often the Winter-man—serve the purpose of drawing attention to the dualities that are an inevitable part of the experience of migration, particularly from a landscape and a cultural as well as physical climate that is decidedly different from Canada's:

> How he plunged bravely
> from sun to snow
> made the perfect metaphor
> from elephant and ice,
> the breath of his sun children,
> but never stepped out of the womb.
> (*EI* 127)

Ten poems in this collection belong to this category and function as a convenient shorthand to transform the private into the public and emphasize an allegorical dimension to a cross-cultural encounter. Judith Miller rightly maintains that "the dualities blend and invade each other in unexpected ways, in poems of warning, challenge and affirmation."[15] The Sun-man is both the poet and not the poet. In lines such as:

> I saw him today,
> in a skullcap of snow,
> crawling into his apartment
> to survive
> on ready-to-serve oatmeal
> (*EI* 21)

the distance is established, almost as if to prevent a solipsism that could degenerate into an excess of emotion. It also becomes a way of ironizing his own predicament, of showing the multiple facets of his experience.

The preoccupation with the Sun-man begins early in *Flesh and Thorn* and persists even in his most recent *Beatitudes of Ice*, although the treatment of the personal is often more complex and nuanced in his recent poetry. Poems such as "Don't tell me" and the poems that proclaim the beauty of the raven are all part of this public persona that negotiates the difficult terrain of past and present. Practically every volume is a gesture or a stance—oppositional, elegiac or placatory—and the rain and the raven are reflections and facets of the Sun-man. But the volume that reinforces this binary and makes it its primary concern is *Elephant and Ice*, where even the cover, which depicts an elephant standing in a sea of dissolving ice, draws attention to the thematic preoccupation. Uma Parameswaran is among those who have provided a detailed and perceptive reading of the twin forms of elephant and ice. Several of the other poems in this collection reinforce the paradigm established by the persona.

From the opening poem in *Elephant and Ice* about origins and the prophecy of migration, to the last poem which adopts an attitude of reconciliation to the present, the poems move almost teleologically through a variety of experiences describing the contraries of East and West. "Immigrant," for instance, sets up the wild lilies and weeds on the one hand and "white silence of civilization" on the other. Some of the most exciting poems that Crusz has written in the last twenty years have grown out of this sense of exile. "After the Snowfall" in *Beatitudes* is a splendid evocation of the predicament of alienation, captured in a cluster of metaphors that is visual, seasonal and mythical. The poem is an example of his more recent poetry where the theme comes across in a more restrained and artistically complex manner.

The ethnic dimension invites the label "immigrant poet" and links this body of poetry to a whole genre of postcolonial poems, notable examples of which are Soyinka's "Telephone Conversation"[16] and more recently Arnold Itwaru's "Arrival"[17] and Dabydeen's "Coolie Son."[18] It also invites a whole range of questions about nostalgia, exoticism, essentialism, hyperbole and caricature. The poet becomes a "public" figure in these poems, leading to generalizations of various sorts. Margaret Atwood, in a generally positive appraisal in a letter, is nonetheless a bit perplexed by Crusz's tendency to use images that do not make sense to a Western reader. In a letter dated 23 May 1971, she maintains that an "excessive use of local place names etc . . . can come out sounding like a parody of Kipling."[19] Crusz himself recalls that journals have on occasion refused his poems on the grounds that they are too exotic. In fact, in a poem Crusz admits that

They will not, cannot
hear another song,
or read maps
to my island
in the sun
(*EI* 92)

The road that Crusz tries to chart is a particularly complex one that needs to be seen as only partially involved with multicultural issues. In several of his poems, he is concerned with issues such as racism, as in "After the K-W Writer's Award" and his more recent poetry. In these poems the binary stance is particularly significant. It recognizes that ethnicity determines or overrides other considerations. That the theme has not been exorcised is evident in two of his unpublished poems, one set in a church where an old lady refuses to shake hands with him and another in which the Sun-man encounters in Toronto's Chinatown two skinheads who taunt him with racist insults. The effect of this unprovoked insult is echoed in the halting, deliberate movement of the poem. In yet another poem he targets academics who "fix" him in a stereotype and provoke in him a gesture of rebellion. Here one sees the attitude of defiance that W M Verhoeven refers to when he says that "in any multicultural society, the minority culture must be ready to write itself into being in the face of a hegemonic culture that will continually attempt to unwrite it."[20]

More significantly, the binary is constructed in a manner that reveals a deliberate imbalance. The elephant and ice are not on an equal plane, although as metonyms they serve an allegorical purpose. The ice is real to an extent that the elephant is not, although the poet does in fact insist that elephants are equally real. The distinction lies in the fact that ice is part of the referential world of Canada, from ice-skating to snow-shovelling. The elephant is part of a remembered reality in that it is more important not as part of the landscape as much as the subjectivity associated with Sri Lanka. When Catherine Ahearn in a letter maintains that "the elephant is . . . a kind of super animal"[21] she is in fact identifying the mythical and metaphoric dimension of the image. It is deliberately metaphoric, almost self-consciously so, not in the way that Ondaatje sees the landscape of Sri Lanka in *Running in the Family*. To remember elephants as tourists do, of the procession of elephants in the Perahera in Kandy, is to fuel an exotic vision of a particular kind. To describe elephants the way Crusz does is to evoke a worldview, one that can only be relived through such metaphors.

Huggan makes this distinction very clear when he says: "The otherness of ethnicity is the result of a lived experience: it corresponds to the daily reality of those who inhabit the social margins. Ethnicity often bespeaks some form of social disadvantage; the negotiation of otherness has its basis in survival. The otherness of exoticism, by contrast, involves a search for imaginary alternatives."[22] Regardless of the issues raised by the comment, the crucial point is that such a division does exist, and "exoticism" needs to be contextualised carefully. Thus at one level Crusz might appear ethnic and at another exotic, although the main purpose is not always subversion or valorization.

Crusz's concern with the two worlds is largely subjective and has to be seen in terms that are not exclusively political. The evocation is both referential and fictive in that Crusz shuttles between a response to verifiable realities and imaginary ones. And that is precisely why even the description of an alienating Canadian landscape is described in images that are aesthetically compelling. By the same token, the description of Sri Lanka can be negative and can be the subject of scathing irony. Here, for instance, is a stanza from "Dark Antonyms in Paradise":

> Five-star hotels now gleam
> in the Sri Lanka sun, tourists
> dip their bottoms
> in the everlasting blue
> of your circling sea, wrap
> the pink skins in cotton and silks,
> the loud embrace of batik;
> and your craft boutiques burst
> at their seams with elephant and ivory,
> the filigree effusions
> of your artistic people.
> (*SW* 51)

To reject these poems on the premise that these are not in the strict sense "Canadian" or to valorize them on the premise that they represent the true voice of Caliban is only partially valid. They lead to dichotomies that are disturbing. The danger here is that of orientalising the two worlds where the East becomes a paradise and West a negation of spontaneity and joy. Why, for instance, is the East seen as a place

> where the palms bend
> their coconut breasts
> to the morning sun,
> and Nuwera-Eliya's valley
> oozes with the fragrance of tea
> (*EI* 36),

while the West is presented as a place where

> . . . the children
> split their brains
> with Mattel's TV toys,
> and Aunt Melissa
> comes back to life
> with her two-dollar animal card.
> (*EI* 86)

How different is the description of Sri Lanka from orientalist views? Is Tapping not accurate when he says that Crusz's "assertions are untested and too often pietistic, the claims are much too grand and thus naive, and the writing is too frequently unconsciously bathetic."[23] How does one respond to Sugunasiri's contention that "his poems are strewn with references to the sun, tropical fruits, birds and fish, and a local celebration or two. But these are also, by and large, the ones that any tourist would be attracted to. All this, unfortunately, is 'song and dance'."[24] Crusz very self-consciously evokes these images, of landscape, of animals and birds, the rivers and the sea, partly because these were realities that he grew up with, both in Galle and in Dehiwela. His brother Noel speaks about the experience of beachcombing in his article on Hilary.[25] Rienzi mentions in conversation how from his home in Dehiwela, he saw elephants on almost a daily basis being taken to the river and the paddy fields that were a part of the landscape he grew up in. But such remembered realities also function in the poetic world as tropes for subjective positions.

Sugunasiri does not allow for heterogeneity and Tapping does not acknowledge artifice readily enough. That such extreme positions are possible is curious but not altogether surprising given the current tendency to reinforce the referent in postcolonial studies. It is, however, important to remember that any attempt to "fix" the meaning of the poetry in a preconceived scheme is likely to distort the overall preoccupation of the author. To insist that certain perspectives are somehow more worthy than others is to run the risk of recapitulating the same fallacies that the poet is accused of. For Crusz the landscape, the animals and the birds are all part of a constructed system that captures his subjective response to the country. There is in fact no bathos but elegiac meditation, no "song and dance" but simply song. He maintains that what the poetry does is "recreate the fiction of the country [he] had lost."[26] It is the constructedness of this world that becomes the subject of his poem "Memory's Truth," where he admits,

As for the monsoon rain,
there'll only be the beautiful slant
of raindrops,
cool massage,
me dancing naked
under God's own shower head;
And the havocking floods,
mud huts dissolving like chocolate?

bloated bodies
riding the dark currents to the sea?

I wouldn't know.
(*EI* 17)

It is also important to remember that while the Sun-man readily lends itself to a form of overt valorization, the image of the raven is in fact the opposite. When a poem claims that the raven is God in disguise, the poet is making both a spiritual and a political point. Thus a deliberate destabilization of orientalist images too must be taken into consideration even as one deals with binary formulations. And in the title *The Rain Doesn't Know Me Any More* is implied a gradual distancing, an awareness that time and distance have created changes that an overly simple identification could not acknowledge.

More significantly, these are the tropes that enable the poet to capture the lyricism that attests to his attachment to the country. Where the personal is a cause for pain, and the political is a reminder of otherness, the landscape, as in Walcott, becomes a way of defining one's identity and one's roots. It allows for the expression of a lyricism, of a mood that is otherwise difficult to capture. Rhythm is central to Crusz's poetry, in the patterns of repetition, the stress, the alliteration, and the lush landscape with its proliferation of imagery allows for the haunting rhythms.

Crusz himself is aware of the dangers of idealizing the past and creating a neat dichotomy that simplifies an obviously complex experience. In those self-deprecatory gestures where he refers to himself as one

bound in cap and bells,
a dusky clown
beating winter's silence
to a bellyfull of laughter
(*EI* 37)

he is aware that such dualities do serve only a limited purpose. He recognizes that such dualities smack of artifice when they are used to make simplistic assertions about two nations. Such poems have an allegorical function and work with a complex interplay of multiple positions that both affirm and deny the validity of mutually exclusive points of view.

In fact it is this awareness of slipping into what might well seem essentialist statements that appears to be the basis of the poem "but seek the road" where he talks about "crows/that permute common dark moods,/angular flights unworthy of netting." But his imagination is drawn to the mango leaf, its death, and the "tree smiling at its roots/for a death/so exotically done" (*EI* 52). The so-called exotic thus feeds the imagination and provides the tropes that define a state of mind. The very term "exotic" occurs repeatedly in Crusz, and for him the connotations are of exuberance caused by the memory of a once-familiar landscape rather than a form of essentialism.

It is probably also the consciousness of an over-schematic delineation that leads in the later poems in the volume and in other poems to a reconciliation, where he establishes a balance between the two worlds:

> A brown laughing face
> in the snow,
> not the white skull
> for the flies
> in Ceylon's deadly sun.
> (*EI* 95)

Here the images are a reminder of the harshness—political and social as much as climatic—of Sri Lanka against which the juxtaposition of laughter and snow seems much more acceptable.

Equally important is the fact that several of the poems hardly parade a simple duality. Even in poems that deal with familiar themes about the West—materialism, artificiality, alienation—the context is rendered ambivalent. In "Civilization" (*RD* 11) the irony of seeking out discount items and hankering after the "second cup free" and the absurdity of rushing to parking lots like animals at some "African watering hole" does not exclude from its irony the author, who is himself seduced by the moment. And he ends the poem on a self-reflexive note:

> All this metaphor
> for nothing
> but food, clothing and shelter?
> (*RD* 12)

Even when the objective is to lament the diasporic predicament, the sheer image-making power of the poetry remains a stay against a simple duality. The creative energy that drives the poem aestheticises what could be a bleak experience. Parameswaran rightly points out that "his imagery continues to be a marvellous conjugation of Canadian and Sri Lankan landscapes, of the elephant and woodapple dreams on the banks of the Mahaveli mingling with the snowbanks of this 'marshmallow land.' "[27]

And by the same token, his treatment of Sri Lanka is not complimentary at all times. If the past that is evoked through Sardiel—the folk hero and Robin Hood figure of Sri Lanka—expresses admiration and empathy with resistance, the poems that deal with the militancy of the Tamil Tigers show both a sense of distancing and a sense of the ironic. In both there is the consciousness that the fiction of Sardiel he celebrates is more important than the referential world. In "Dark Antonyms" there is once more the consciousness that the narratives of nationalism that the government has painstakingly created have not been able to eclipse the suffering of the people.

Crusz recalls when several of his poems were rejected on the grounds that they were too exotic that he wrote "Remains of an Oriental Poet Writing in Canada" (*EI* 87), a poem that exemplifies the spare line, curbs any suggestion of emotional excess and emerges as a tightly-constructed poem. Such poems that resist referentiality and stress artifice are significant, but in very different ways. And when he writes poems that are distinctly imagistic and minimalist, as in "Resurrection" the effect is not as satisfying as in the poems of intense emotion and excess.

What distinguishes the "ethnic" poems that work well with these dualities is the quality of imagery that several poets, including Ghose, have drawn attention to: the capacity to create, through striking metaphors, the sense of seeing anew. Ghose mentions, for instance, the notion of "batik exuberance" where the combination has the effect of transforming the quotidian into something delightful.[28] Sometimes it is the textual universe, the association of images within the poem that creates the lyricism of the poems. He is aware, as in "The Interview" how easily these attempts can be misread as simplistic assertions about Canada and Sri Lanka. And yet one needs to be aware of the distinction between a poem that is explicitly referential and one that seeks complex formal configurations.

In many respects, the counterpart of the poems like "Summertime in Waterloo Park," which satirise the various "rituals" induced by the salubrious weather, are ones like the "Sacred Cow" (*EI* 66-67) which reflect on the failure of religion; the latter, although set in India, draws attention to issues of class, of poverty, of the misuse of religion, and so on, which are insistently realistic. It is the absence of this level of social consciousness that Tapping castigates in his review. Such poems have a relevance and a purpose that anyone can identify and relate to. And these poems are closer in spirit and method to the poems set in Canada where the social dimension, where the impact on daily life is felt in concrete terms. But realism also leads to a tendentious quality, a preachiness that is absent in his best poems. The poet's intention is to capture states of mind and it is in his capacity to create a cluster of images suggesting states of mind that he excels. An overt tendentious quality, even in superbly crafted poems like "Sermon in the Forest" (*EI* 68-70), is not as effective.

Where images fail to capture the imagination, where images seem to be either far-fetched or hackneyed, the poems lose their impact. It is important to remember that Crusz left the country because of a failed marriage. He also left because the politics of the country were moving in a direction that was hardly conducive to the Burghers. Of these the former becomes the basis of his love poems. The Sun-man poems reach towards a deeper dimension, a sense of harmony that he associates with his childhood, with his family, with an aspect of the land that transcends individual acts of betrayal. The poet is aware that memory distorts and what the creative impulse shapes so carefully may be no more than a figment of the imagination. He claims:

> I know. I'll make the coconut tree
> forever straight,
> without hint of midnight beetle   deep
> in the pink fruit's throat
> (*BI* 17)

But the distortion is part of the process of creating a textual universe which is only intermittently referential but one that preserves a sense of harmony, one in which the tensions of the present do not exist.

The two worlds of Canada and Sri Lanka, in all their complexity, are germane to his writing. They do not make up the totality of his corpus but they are a constitutive aspect of his work. He is aware that he could have avoided them in favour of a world that locates itself on the global cusp and denies nationalist borders. In a recent unpublished poem entitled "Trick with a Knife" he intertextually recalls the mode of Ondaatje, not with the "anxiety of influence" but with good natured repartee. He realizes that to mimic Ondaatje is to court disaster. He must remain in his own world.

Critical exegesis has, unfortunately, been less concerned with the middle ground, although critics have, in fact, at various times alluded to the power of synthesis. Thorpe, in a review of *The Rain*, comments that "Sri Lanka glows vividly in him . . . yet with a clear sense of the limitations of the picturesque idyll . . . "[29] And Mukherjee observes that "at his best Crusz blends his Sri Lankan and Canadian experiences to make profound comments on both societies."[30] The movement from one trope to the other is always contingent, fluid and indeterminate. It finds metaphoric expression in "Faces of the Sun-Man":

He is a body
of blue water
shaped like a man,
limpid to the depths;
you can look or move
into him, through him,
the fluid dimension holds.
(*EI* 34)

The contrasting landscapes are part of a total body of knowledge he draws on to reveal the human dimension of the predicament of exile. When Arnold Itwaru in a letter of 28 September 1989 speaks of "the beauty and pathos of a life on a universal yet alien shore"[31] this is exactly what he pays tribute to.

It is not without significance that the title of his recent collection is *Beatitudes of Ice*. Although the phrase itself occurs in a context that renders it ironic, the thrust of several poems in this volume is towards balance and acceptance. If not for the poet, at least for the son,

Home is where the snowman
sits on the front lawn
and waits patiently
for his return. (*BI* 30-31)

But when the birds are gone, and their warm fields
Return no more, where, then, is paradise?

"Sunday Morning"—WALLACE STEVENS[1]

IV. A DEATH SO EXOTICALLY DONE

The notion of an "immigrant" poet concerned with the dynamics of exile suggests a certain sociological relevance and urgency, which is as true of Crusz as it is of several other so-called hyphenated Canadian poets. In the case of Crusz the label has persisted, partly because the cluster of images he has used to define the dichotomies has had an enduring appeal, and partly because the personal predicament has served so well for him as a synecdoche for the cultural conflicts of South Asians. And since he has never really abandoned this preoccupation, and since the literary climate in Canada is receptive to such writing, this aspect has also had the effect of eclipsing the multiple themes which run through his work and deemphasizing the subtle orchestration of the fictive and the referential in his poetry.

It is not often recognized that the first volume of poems was almost entirely concerned with the pain of betrayal and the assertion of self in the face of personal tragedy. As his poem "The Roses Are the Color of Blood" (*SW* 64) so effectively points out, the inspiration behind his poetry was his love for the woman who deserted him. In unrhymed couplets, this poem demonstrates the complex relation between the two. The first collected volume published by *TSAR* entitled *A Time for Loving* reinforces, significantly, the concern with love—a point that is made forcefully in the introduction by Reshard Gool and also in Crusz's essay "Talking about Myself." Even the poems that are ostensibly about migration—poems such as "Little Brown Boy"— have more to do with love than about marginality. Admittedly, this poem's intertextual connection with Blake's "Little Black Boy" and the striking juxtapositions in the first two stanzas have to do with notions of otherness, but the end of the poem shifts its focus to the poet's sense of guilt and the pain of his children in the personal tragedy. The benediction with which the poem closes is again a statement about love:

> And you slept on.
> defying
> emptiness,
> closing my silent wound
> (*FT*, n.p.)

A number of poems in *Flesh and Thorn* recall the raw pain of betrayal. But strangely enough, several of his finest poems have to do with the celebration of love, not merely the pain and dislocation it caused in his life. Layton was among the first to speak of this quality in his early poems, where the exuberance of passion is flaunted with little restraint.[2] There are times when passion slips into sentimentality and when the emotion appears to be excessive and self-indulgent, but for the most part, what comes across is the intensity of feeling, as when he speaks of the woman

> who once set fire to wet grass
> with torches in your limbs,
> coaxed suns like butterflies
> on to your open palms,
> spoke words as passionate
> as elephants trumpeting the moon?
> (*FT* n.p.)

In the more recent love poems to Anne the passion is held in check and the tone is more serene, but the celebration of love remains intrinsic to his poetry and his sensibility.

Contrary to this celebration is the sense of nightmare in the poem "Before My Birthday" where the real and the dreamlike merge to produce an image of desolation. The effect is surrealistic, bringing together a range of emotions, bordering on hysteria. Sometimes the Romantic impulse of "spontaneous overflow of powerful emotions" is deflected in the metaphor, and a more modernist tendency to distance the author and encapsulate the emotion in metaphor is evident. In such poems the intentional element recedes to the background, but the emotion is still very much an important presence.

From his very first poem in *Flesh* which speaks, in wonderfully modulated sexual terms, about the pain of love, to the last poem in

Beatitudes that deals with the skill of learning "to dance in the rarefied air" there is a multiplicity that is crucial to understanding his work. As he moves from one volume to the next, the patterns of emphasis change, the range of subject matter alters, and he begins to acquire different strengths. To see him in relation to a few persistent themes is inevitably problematic.

A recent poem called "Homecomings" employs the striking phrase "an umbrella of doting children" to refer to his deep commitment to his children and their role in preserving his stability. Almost all the poems in the section titled "Government by Soother" in *Still Close to the Raven* are about the enduring love for his children. At its most poignant, poems like "Son" are a reminder of how children transform agony caused by the vicissitudes of life into philosophical acceptance. At the other end of the spectrum are the playful poems that add a dimension of humour to an otherwise alienating circumstance or feed into an elegiac impulse about Sri Lanka. Hence the poems about Michael in relation to the Singhala ears or the ones that lament he is "free from history's pain" or that he would not know what it means to be a farmer in Sri Lanka. What often distinguishes these poems is that the children's poems are an occasion not merely to write reflectively, but to write with the apparent artlessness that becomes a child. Irony, understatement and mockery are all part of the emotional gamut of these poems where, for instance, the innocent questioning of a child can well become the occasion for self-reflexivity. These poems also provide the context to introduce rhythms of speech that retain their colloquial element and enable the intersection of Sri Lankan and Canadian idioms.

As in Yeats's "A Prayer for My Daughter," where the child triggers a meditative mood, the child remains a symbolic presence, and the function of the poem is to reflect on very different—existential—concerns. In that wonderfully ironic poem called "Baby-Photo Inc. vs Michael Egerton Crusz" Crusz's infant son's capacity to subvert the claims of "art" with rebellious tears prompts the poet to speculate on issues relating to identity:

> Without the genetic dream,
> Perahera, sand crab, castle,
> the drumbeat of our mongrel blood,
> of history made, undone,

in some far green island home,
you are no more exotic
than Vancouver crow.
(*SW* 17)

As against these are the poems that are more specifically about the children, where the tone, rhythm and the actual context establish a direct relation with the object of the poetry.

While the children's poems are both ironic and elegiac, the ones written for his parents and his brother are uniformly adulatory. The relation between the two alerts the reader to changes wrought by time, by conventions, and by migration. To juxtapose the two is to see in stark contrast two very different value systems. The attitude of the poet to his children is a shifting one, moving from love and humour to irony and mild censure. For the parents, the poet has nothing but absolute admiration. If the notion of a praise poem is applied to lyrics, it would particularly apply to ones that he writes for his parents and his brother. A comparison between the article written by his brother Noel on the death of Hilary entitled "A Don's Journey to God" and his own poem called "Elegy for an Elder Brother" (*RD* 66) that utilises religious imagery provides a sense of how the poetic transforms the referential to suggest layers of meaning. The elegies written for his father, the mathematician and teacher, and for his mother, the disciplinarian and artist, evoke a way of life that is in contrast to the more satirical contemporary poems and the more allegorical nature poems. To read the elegies is to get a sense of what it meant to be growing up in a conservative household in the thirties, the curious mixture of influences that characterised pre-independent Sri Lanka. To read these poems is also to understand the admixture of precision and emotion that appears in the best of Crusz's work.

Crusz's brother Hilary was a lay apostle and his brother Noel was for some time a priest. His father was closely associated with the Jesuits and Crusz himself is a staunch Catholic. Hence the large number of religious poems written by him. Here again, as in the love poems, what strikes the reader is the range of responses to religion and God, from the solemnity of "The Accepted One" to the levity of "Yes, in My Fathers's House There Are Many Rooms." "The Accepted One" is a particularly important poem, not only because it received honourable mention in a competition soon after it was published by

Grail, but also because it was written in the context of his brother's decision to leave the Church. It is a poem about faith, about grace, about the need to be true to one's own self, and having expressed the sanctimonious outrage of the religious community, the poem ends with the memorable lines, "And God does not pitch his thoughts/in the dark Sun." While the solemn poems are significant, in general, what are most striking are those that combine a religious sensibility with a tone which, in its irreverence and humour, is as close to the Metaphysical poets as they are to Hindu *Bhakti* literature. Although there is very little in his own work—apart from the occasional reference to Tagore—to establish the direct influence of Hindu literature, it is highly unlikely that he would have remained untouched by the presence of Hinduism in Sri Lanka. Robert Crusz ends his essay with the comment that "[Rienzi] was also brought up in the multi-religious environment of Sri Lanka and every day came face-to-face with the other great religions of the world—Buddhism, Hinduism and Islam."[3]

In fact the irrepressible humour of his children's poetry finds its way into his religious poetry. In poems such "Yes, in My Father's . . ."—a hilarious light-hearted poem that satirises the materialism of institutionalised religion—the relation between the God and the devotee takes on different facets. To ask for a "24-inch TV" is to position oneself as a child and to speak to God with the kind of familiarity and intimacy that one often encounters in *Bhakti* literature. Very much along the same lines "God in the Apple Turnover" speaks of God stealing the cricket ball to play for a few moments by himself, an attitude that bears a striking resemblance to Saivaite poetry.

But there is also a serious—and referential—aspect to the religious poetry, which explains his moral indignation when he encounters racism in a church. The exuberance of his other religious poems is noticeably absent in this one where the couplet restricts the movement of the poem and the very economy reinforces the shock of experiencing blatant racism in the church. The unrhymed couplets are ideally suited for understatement and that makes the satirical and vituperative quality of the poem all the more forceful. Significantly titled " 'Let us now/ in the embracing love of the Father,/ Wish each other/ The Peace of Christ'—Pastor Malone of St Michael's" the poem then states:

So, my brown hand stretches
to the old lady standing beside me.

She turns and glares, then extends
a thin pale index finger.

I accept this synecdoche of brotherhood,
and shake hands with a finger,

still believing, refusing to snuff out
the last candle to our darkness.

More effective, perhaps, is the allegorical "Lion and the Crow," an unpublished poem in which the metaphors both distance and render more complex the experience. As the crow lies unconscious after being attacked by an offended and quick-tempered lion, God, in the midst of operating on the crow, offers words of advice in a manner that recalls Blake's tiger and the lamb while giving this encounter a contemporary relevance:

You fool,
who lulls an ant to sleep
under an elephant's foot?
Yes. I certainly made crow
bold, black and mouthy,
but also a shimmering shadow
against the sun.

And you I made
king of the beasts,
though with some severe disabilities:
like getting your wife to hunt
for your meals, an attitude problem,
and far too much of siesta
under the acacia tree.

The award he won in a contest in Waterloo testifies to the strength of his religious poems, particularly those that appear in *Still Close, The Rain* and *Beatitudes*. That he could write these poems within the context of a secular imagination is unusual in Canadian, or for that matter, postcolonial writing. Unlike, say, the religious poetry of Christopher Okigbo, which draws so heavily from indigenous mythical traditions, Crusz's poetry is at its best when the religious sensibility merges with the ebb and flow of natural phenomena. The religious poems are, for the most part, Christian, with occasional departures into Buddhism and Hinduism. The "Sermon in the Forest" has very obvious Christian connotations, but it remains distinctly Buddhist in its philosophical assumptions.

The Hindu poem—the only one in his entire corpus—is an unusual one, for obvious reasons set in India rather than in Sri Lanka. In it the poet explores the complex intersection of caste, class and religious practice in a manner that stresses sociological relevance. Probably because in Sri Lanka Buddhism, and to a lesser extent Hinduism, have played a crucial and sometimes deciding role in the politics of ethnic struggle, the poet steers clear of direct reference to the role of religion; for the same reasons that he chooses not to dwell on the politics of the country, he also opts to distance himself from religious satire. More secure in dealing with his own religion, he writes with the confidence of an insider, adopting a filial mode that, surprisingly, draws its inspiration from a Hindu mode.

All these are about issues that concern the poet, and they are not without significance. But to stress them in isolation is also to underscore the notion of poetry as a vehicle for ideas. Where Crusz has focused on the tendentious, the poetry has had the effect of acquiring a turgid quality. In a recent letter, Ghose rightly expresses his reservation about lines such as:

What is bare and empty
remains bare and empty
only if the mind lets go
the continuing dream. . .[4]
(*BI* 8)

where the poem gives the impression of gathering momentum until it reaches that point of explication. Here the poetic element recedes to the background and the message dominates the poem. The narrative and linear quality rather than the metaphoric and synchronic one accounts for the movement of the poem and that weakens the overall effect. Always conscious of living in a culture that is increasingly sensitive to the provisionality of truths, Crusz, at his best, avoids the "message-driven" poem.

When the poem relies on a closure that gains its strength from outside rather than from within itself, it lends itself to what Veronica Forrest-Thomson rightly calls "bad naturalisation."[5] Here the strength of the poem diminishes in proportion to the extent to which it relies on the external world to explicate its meaning. Forrest-Thomson sees that as a dominant weakness in Larkin and about Larkin's poetry says: "his technique is exact, if unexciting; it fulfils the reader's expectations, leading him to think of it once more. But it does no more than that. It leaves poetry stranded on the beach of the already-known world, to expand and limit itself there."[6] Calling this habit a "form of insincere calculation" Jonathan Holden, in his discussion of the lyric, refers to this mode as the "heresy of explicitness."[7]

In the kind of poems that Crusz writes, particularly the meditative ones in which the speaker alone dominates the poem and the listener is no more than a token presence, the message is central. It is probably less so in those that establish a more complex pattern of persona, listener and reader where the statements are qualified or framed by ironic asides. But even among those where only the speaker's voice is heard, at their best the poems create a system that foregrounds the artifice and makes the meaning contingent on the various structures that operate within the poem itself.

The poem that begins *Flesh and Thorn* has often been interpreted as a love poem—framed by imagery that is distinctly sexual. And that in fact is true:

> The way
> the Ceylonese farmer
> husks the coconut:
> a crowbar planted
> and the iron tooth
> jabs the skin;
> the flesh tears
> till the bone shows
> round and clean;
> the hammer of machete
> on the skull,
> the milk leaks
> and the sweet kernel opens out
> like a womb.
> (*FT* n.p.)

The emotion that prompts the poem is a personal one, and as the rest of the poem makes clear, the poem is at least partly about the violence associated with love. The central metaphor that captures the aggressive sexuality of the poem belongs to the world of the Sri Lankan villager, for whom the business of husking coconuts is a routine activity. For the villager, husking a coconut is a necessary act of economic need and survival. Without the paradoxical force it acquires within the poem, the metaphor could well become exotic. It is quite possibly not something that an urban poet could claim as part of his life. The "hammer of machete" and the "sweet kernel" opening out like a womb are a curious juxtaposition that reminds the reader of the artifice of poetic construction. The diction of the poem itself eschews conventional poetic diction and tries to approximate ordinary speech. And yet the metaphor draws the reader back into the poem, preventing the "didactic heresy" (to use Holden's term). It is the play of different structures that defamiliarises the experience and gives the poem its particular strength. As Chamberlin points out, "the experiences of life are realized in the elements and forms of art—circles, centers, patterns, rhythms, rituals—which in turn represent relationships between our ordinary selves and greater powers, part of nature and part of us."[8]

There is always in Crusz an awareness that the imagination transforms the real into constructs; and despite the referentiality of his work, at some level he lives in a textual universe and works within its parameters. He recognizes the inner need to create schematic worlds, but as Ghose points out in a strikingly similar poem entitled "A Memory of Asia,"[9] these are inventions. As Crusz says,

> There's a raging moon,
>   the fruit bat's nightly orgy is on;
> but cadju pulang and mango
>   will still be whole and sweet.
> (*BI* 17)

And within those terms of love and despair,

> the green land
> forever green,
> the lost country
> ever perfect.

This Keatsian response is as much about his own poetry as it is about the experience. And the self-reflexivity is a constant stay against any form of excess.

Singing Against the Wind begins a poem entitled "The Elephant Who Would Be a Poet" that serves as an apologia for his poetry and as an illustration of the thematic and formal preoccupations that run through his work. It is an example of the short, carefully structured, tonally perfect meditative poem he often writes and that allows for the precise articulation of a deeply felt experience. This is one of the many poems about the process of writing poetry, about the isolation of the poet from those around him, told through the image of an elephant and his mahout. After a day of tiring and monotonous logging, the elephant decides to relax in a most perplexing manner:

Without command
he eases his huge body to the ground
rolls over,
makes new architecture
from his thick legs,
four columns vertical
to the sun.

Predictably, the mahout is taken by surprise and is confused by the display:

The confused mahout
refuses the poem
in this equilibrium
this crazy theatre of the mind
(*SW* 9)

In another poem, the poet returns to the elephant image, and here a reader is enticed by the pervasive presence of the elephant to give a "tiny crystal elephant" as a Christmas gift to the poet. Wanting to pursue the relation between symbol and substance, the poet probes further about the reader's response and is advised to look again at the elephant. He does and "a very lopsided beast/was staring at him with curious eyes" (*BI* 57). Removed from a system of which it is a part, the beast looks awkward and exoticised, the symbol inappropriate, comic and irrelevant. Time and again, he is aware of the "new architecture" as a problematic one.

In almost every volume, but with increasing frequency in more recent work, self-reflexivity becomes an essential component, as the poet tries to come to terms with his own craft. Particularly in *Beatitudes*, such poems are central to the volume. In the poem "After the K-W Writer's Award" about the recognition he received from his community, he is aware of the hidden agendas that abound and he ends on a note of resignation:

How this woman sidles up
and asks: "Where are you from?"

Soft baby blues (mask green,
hate, as in hooded clansman)

search for fault lines
in my skin, black eyes.

Sorry, lady, I have nothing
but the sweetness of silence,

I've already done
with my fire and my song
(*BI* 65)

Ultimately, it is not the range, not the intensity of feeling, and not even the voice of the other that accounts for the strength of Crusz's poetry. It lies in the capacity to write the short, intense lyric with the exactitude of observation, the strength of metaphor, the gift of perceiving the unusual in the familiar. As in "Fresh-cut Flowers," each stanza is carefully controlled to reveal the complex relation between pain and aestheticism. It reveals the balance he strives to maintain between the experience and the poetry. The poetry also serves as a reminder that the aesthetic and the referential cannot be mutually exclusive. To ignore the real is to recapitulate a decadent aestheticism which goes against the grain of so much of his poetry.

Emotional excess is constantly kept at bay—distanced through metaphor. Stressing the aesthetic does not amount to retreating from the experiential dimension of life; rather, it is to recognize that poetry works with discontinuity, with the careful orchestration of emotion and reason that Keats referred to as "negative capability." Artifice enables the coexistence of contraries, distils the emotions in order to create the possibility of a fruitful tension. About contraries, the poet says:

Only by dying
do we learn the true rhythms
of the heart, by crying,
how to laugh from the belly.
(*RD* 5)

And this movement from one to another is made possible by the artifice of his poetry.

Thorpe, in a recent review, speaks of the need to record the poetry of Crusz, thereby drawing attention to the oral quality of his writing.[10] While the comment is a perceptive one, it is all the more surprising in a body of poetry that at first glance reveals none of the qualities that would lend themselves to oral performance. Patterns of repetition, refrains, the spoken idiom or dialect are rarely conspicuous in his work, except, perhaps, for the poems set in the Caribbean. What he writes is not communal poetry; it is, rather, the assertion of an individual voice, inspired at times by orality.

Crusz hardly conforms in his writing to traditional prosodic patterns, despite a very conventional training and a partiality for traditional iambic patterns. There are moments when his poetry comes close to rhyming couplets or, as in the poem "Prayer" the patterns of a sonnet, but even so neither the end rhyme nor the beat lends itself to an easy identification. And yet rhythm is central to the movement of his poetry, to accessing the emotions that go with his lyrics. As in the last stanza of "Song of Myself" in *Beatitudes*, it is a combination of line length and stress pattern that ensures the rhythmic—almost Whitmanesque—quality.

But have you shared
the pain
in the shattered bird,
the silence
of the thorn that guards the rose?
(*BI* 38)

Here one notices the dominant iambic beat with the exception of the third and final lines where stress pattern alters. The line length of the second and fourth lines ensure a semantic parallel where the trochee suggests the parallel between the guardian and the victim. It is a stanza about which Ghose in a letter quite rightly points out that the metaphor of the rose is too conventional to be totally effective, but one can hardly miss the almost perfect orchestration of rhythm to reveal how free verse can be used for wonderful ends.

Another triumph along these lines is "After the Snowfall" in *Beatitudes* where the conventional concerns with otherness, exoticism, binaries, etc. become less important than the sheer beauty of every line. It is a poem that deserves to be quoted in full for its visual effect to be felt. Here the contemporary experience of migration fuses with the Biblical and the personal becomes the universal.

> Through garage door lookouts,
> winter-hazed:
>
> bleached bones   the catalpa
> (without   its green crinoline head)
>
> King maple so humbled
> frail white arms skying
>
> a tree
> praying for its life
>
> Driveway   divided
> snow walls on either side
>
> the Red Sea parted again
> and Moses   nowhere in sight
>
> But Pharaoh on his snowplough
> continues history: walls the last exit,
>
> laughs: there shall be no diaspora today!
>
> O Lord, mine are summer eyes—
> tomorrow   the promised land?
>
> your Egypt   still shimmers and shines
> in its white   misery
> (*BI* 4)

One is struck by the visual effect of the poem, a quotidian sight wonderfully captured in the line where the snowplough walls up the driveway in a mock prevention of the exit. The images of death and desolation, of decapitation and apocalypse merge with the dominant metaphor of conquest to suggest a desperate attempt at survival. The military images then give way to Biblical ones and these in turn arrive at the personal. As the emotional momentum of the poem changes, so does the metrical pattern, and the exuberant sibilance of "still shimmers and shines" is offset by the abruptness of "white misery." The manner in which the nonsemantic levels (Forrest-Thomson's phrase) work to exert a centripetal force and the effect caused by the intersection of various discourses create the paradoxical effect of a form working against content. In the process, the poem does not defeat itself; rather, it demonstrates how an old theme of exile, now revisited, provides access to a different dimension of experience.

It is the kind of poem that warns the reader against an over-serious reading of all his poetry. Neither cerebral nor given to excess of feeling he transforms the language to give expression to new ways of feeling. The ability to transform the everyday into the special without losing the sense of urgency is part of the unusual achievement of the poet. Trained very much in the British tradition, he does not share the impulse of, say, Brathwaite to reshape the language to give expression to new forms. And yet his genius lies in his penchant for curious combinations that establish connections in the most unexpected way, particularly for those who understand the context. An example of this would be the second stanza of "Little Brown Boy" where the imagery and the rhythm combine to change the semantic force of the line.

Nor have you lost
those Singhala ears
that like the elephant
hear the wood apple fall
gentle as a raindrop
on the sleeping lotus;
it's the glow in your eyes
at birdsong under snow,
or the drumbeat of ice.
(*FT* n.p.)

The conventional expectations of the reader are disrupted, the imagery defamiliarises the experience without consigning it to a realm of otherness, and the potential of the language is thus enlarged. Had he worked within a totally different idiom, the promise of a rich synthesis would not have been fulfilled. Claiming that the unfamiliarity of the terms he uses is simply a marker of otherness is to create a dichotomy and a chasm that is at best expressive of only a partial truth. Neither the training nor the ancestry of the poet allows for an oppositional stance. That is not to say that the differences are not real. That he has been marginalised hardly needs emphasis. But somewhere, there is a middle ground, a fluidity that the poet captures when he says,

I will not travel again
the separate paths of the sun,
the cruel geography of East and West
(*SW* 53)

The poetics of Crusz is bound to be controversial. Some of his shorter poems are very contemporary in their control, in their approximation to patterns of ordinary speech, where the persona of the author is kept at a distance, where the element of surprise in the imagery is worked into a sense of spontaneous speech. Such poems are almost clinical in their precision and while they have the kind of craftsmanship that Ondaatje displays, that is not the special strength of the poet. In fact, Crusz himself admits to that in an unpublished poem titled "Going for Broke" that invites a comparison with Ondaatje. It is a humorous, self-deprecatory poem about his unwillingness and inability to employ the mode of his compatriot:

I tried "Your Trick with a Knife"

but cut myself badly,
almost bled to death.
Which proves
that you cannot trust
the people you talk to, admire,
laugh with, read or read about.

How dangerous it is
to try
those honoured prescriptions,
without first testing
one's own allergies

For him what works is "batik exuberance" not minimalist, carefully controlled writing.

The "batik exuberance" is difficult to define, although in a general sense it owes its origin to the poetry of Romanticism. Unfashionable as it may sound, his poetry is intentional in its semantics in that the poet is often the subject of his poetry. If the persona that the poet assumes allows for range, it is still difficult to separate the poet from the poems. But unlike the traditional lyric, the absence of formal patterns dispels conventionality in his writing. His poetry is about capturing the qualities of ordinary speech while retaining the echoes of traditional metrical patterns.[11] The rhythm—often of the iambic beat—is almost always present, but the imagery transforms what could be formal into something that creates the illusion of artlessness.

He achieves his finest effects in the longish poem that enables him to work with image clusters and motifs to create patterns of meaning. These provide for the elaboration of a theme along Romantic lines rather than through the fragmentariness of contemporary poetry that requires the reader to make the necessary connections. And the didacticism is questioned, deflected, subverted or enhanced by the rhythms, the tropes, the line lengths that leave an impression of ambivalence and multiplicity on the reader. The narrative element forces closure and often the final lines reinforce that sense of finality. But the poem remains discontinuous in its poetics. Frye rightly points out that the element of discontinuity is central to the lyric,[12] and Crusz, at his best, achieves that combination of narrative and artifice. Closure implies metonymy and a direct relation to the outside world. Discontinuity suggests metaphor and the expression of experience mediated through artifice. And both combine in the poetry to create its texture that Robert Crusz in his essay characterizes as "process" in the work of Rienzi Crusz. And the notion of process is as applicable to the poetics as to the content. Solemn poems coexist with humorous ones, and "ethnic" poems stand alongside ones that have no allusion to race or ethnicity.

The desire to "fashion one's own mythologies" occurs constantly in the poetics of Crusz. While this mythology seeks legitimacy in the referential, at least a part of remaining on the cusp involves the self-referential aspect of his mythology. Thus, for instance, the upside-down elephant creating a new architecture in one poem is not unconnected with the naked pillars in the courtyard in another. And these get connected with similar images which suggest ways of seeing contraries. What is a referential image, and what could well have become an exotic one, could be made textual and within that frame acquire a range of meanings. Thus "Leaving—Michael Style" is connected with "After the Snowfall" and that in turn with "Homecomings"; in all three the metaphor of the prodigal son is invoked to explore notions of identity, home and diaspora.

Given the general tendency to stress the sociological over the aesthetic in critical writing about Crusz, it is probably important to insist that tracing the poetics of his writing would inevitably involve a more hermetic approach that looks at the care with which the personal is balanced with the objective, the emotional with the restrained and, more significantly, the lyrical or conventional with patterns of ordinary speech. None of these makes classification any easier or brings him any closer to contemporary trends in writing poetry. But then his subject matter is hardly mainstream and to access the experience of exile in terms that eschew the personal and referential would be a futile exercise.

For those familiar with indigenous literatures in Sri Lanka the constraints that Crusz works with become immediately clear. Writers using Sinhala or Tamil assume an audience, a whole system of mythology and even a political context that is uppermost in the mind of the nation. Using these languages provides easy access to the demotic and the interplay of the oral and the written. None of these is available to Crusz in quite the same way. But for Crusz it is hardly a matter of choice. The English language is the resource he must work with to give expression to an ontology that is largely Asian. Turning these limitations into strengths, he works with a larger canvas that requires the careful orchestration of the referential and the fictive.

This was at last the last;
this was the limit of motion

"The White River"—EDWARD BRATHWAITE[1]

V. VISIONS, CONFESSIONS AND MEMOIRS

In a study of children's literature in Canada, Elizabeth Waterston makes the important point that when major authors write books for children, those too "should surely be placed within the artist's total creation"[2]—a comment that is particularly applicable not only to the children's stories written by Crusz but also all the prose pieces written during the last twenty years or so that have remained unpublished but are clearly germane to his total oeuvre. If the author has been somewhat diffident about his prose and less willing to discuss it, that is because poetry comes more naturally to him and in that medium he found his distinctive voice very early. The prose pieces have been more sporadic, sometimes too personal and at others too distanced, but they remain central to the larger cultural, political and personal framework within which he writes. And despite the ostensible differences in his prose writings, they all connect in significant ways to complement and enrich the poetry he has written.

As already mentioned, his earliest work—written before he left Sri Lanka—is a children's story entitled "Bumpis, the Magic Elephant," which was probably written in the sixties and has undergone several minor revisions (for instance, the elephant, instead of killing the panther as in the first version, simply gives it a walloping kick in the second) and a complete version with illustrations is among the papers archived in the University of Waterloo library. Originally written as a bedtime story for his children, the story is about the intervention of an elephant with magic powers to transport a poor family of a father and four children to the prosperity of the "land of snows." As allegory and wish-fulfilment, the story is relatively easy to decipher, and if the positioning of "home" as miserable and the "land of snows" as all prosperity is too schematic and at odds with the ambivalence of his poetry, it must be remembered that the story was written in a personal context when departure seemed the only way to come to terms with the tragedy occasioned by the breakdown of his marriage. If the story now looks very "colonial" in its valorization of the west and orientalizing of the east, that again needs to be seen in the context of a desperate need to leave the country. The story remains an early work, but it certainly anticipates his later work, and certainly retains a special place as probably the only work that, in its tone and its diction, specifically targets young readers.

The origins of the story are probably as Eastern as they are Western. Echoes of *Peter Pan* and *The Wizard of Oz* are evident from the beginning. The emphasis on the elephant is a reminder of Babar and his exploits. Here again Waterston is right in her comment that "most authors read and echo the work of writers from other times and places, and literary works are sited internationally and cross-temporally."[3] But the story which is part animal story and part fantasy probably owes much to Indian myth, legends involving the elephant-headed Ganesh, the Buddhist Jataka tales, the festive annual Perahera—the procession of elephants—in Kandy and even the daily spectacle of elephants being taken to the river to be bathed. The symbol of the elephant as a God-like creature with immense strength and patience that runs through his poetry probably begins in this story.

The motif of the journey and the quest is in itself conventional and belongs to a whole group of such stories. Here, the family, at the prompting of the magic elephant, undertakes a one-way journey on the back of the elephant, a journey that takes them through a forest, the sea and finally to the land of the snows. The story is complete with surprises, reversals, dangers, unexpected offers of help, and a closure that resolves the various impediments. The schematic structure of the story is offset by the ambivalence of the forest being the abode of evil panthers and snakes, but also the source of fruits and sustenance. The land the family leaves behind is harsh, but it is also associated with mynah birds and the bird of paradise. The ambivalence that characterizes his poetry is equally true of this story where a measure of indeterminacy renders an otherwise straightforward story complex. And refusal to advance the plot in relation to Manichean oppositions redeems the story from a simple recapitulation of centre and margin.

If the ending is crucial to the story—particularly one that addresses children—so is the leisurely narrative that provides a sensuous description of nature, the world of fruits, flowers, and animals. The two elements—one that celebrates the object of the quest and the other that remembers the land that was left behind—are brought together in the ending which says that the family "lived happily ever after in the land of the snows and whenever the soft white snowflakes fell over the land they always remembered the majestic and kindly elephant—Bumpis" (9).

Despite the personal circumstances that occasioned the story, the displacement is clear enough, for the characters are Sinhalese rather than Burgher, and the family includes a poor villager and his four children. While the absence of a mother in the nuclear family suggests the autobiographical element, the narrative effectively displaces the personal to a plot that is sufficiently distanced to be effective. The story is prophetic, for the chain of events that led to the emigration to Canada were to happen soon, again with that same *deux ex machina* that characterises the story.

While the trope of a journey to another land in search of prosperity is not a popular one in Sri Lanka, the rags-to-riches story, which is at least partly about class—about being transformed from lowly village folk to the nobility that rides on the back of elephants—is not altogether unknown. Unlike traditional children's stories where the wealth is a consequence of chance or moral goodness or piety, the change of fortune in "Bumpis" is a consequence of migration: a concept that was still relatively new in the country. The political backdrop of the story is the exodus in the 1960s of the Burghers, who were forced to migrate to Canada and Australia, and that remains the allegory behind the story.

The story is short, and predictably so because of the absence of detail. The reader is given very little background to place the family, and apart from pieces of information that are gathered through brief descriptions, very little is given to aid a satisfactory referential reading. And this lacuna works suggestively and effectively in a children's story where spatial and temporal dimensions are less important than in a work for adults. As with the poetry, much of the power of the tale comes from the suggestiveness and the narrative structures that are created. Thus the oppositions that are set up—between the sea and the forest, the elephant and the other animals—all provide layers of meaning, which include the notion of class. If, at its most abstract level, the story is about the powers of good and evil, at its most obvious it is about class and poverty, mediated and alleviated by the magic elephant.

The notion of class and the underdog who triumphs is also the impulse behind the discontinuous narrative "Sardiel," a collage of poems, anecdotes, prose pieces, interviews, documentary reports, that create a composite of the legendary Robin Hood figure Sardiel, the champion of the underdog, who (according to legend) lived a charmed life, and who reputedly frustrated the British in the nineteenth century until he was finally betrayed by one of his associates.

The various legends that surround the life of Sardiel are both fascinating and paradoxical. To this day the village where he supposedly lived commemorates his life with lanterns and festivities. In popular myth he is still the folk hero whose magic charms made him virtually impossible to apprehend and legend has it that special measures had to be taken to finally capture this rebel. Such tales are often not interested in shades of grey, and in folk memory he is still the courageous outlaw who, with a few followers, took on the British. As the poem "By Leave of the Gods" claims

> You sang, as would the hunted slave,
> a special song, long,
> mercurial, loud enough
> for every stone to pick up
> the sweet thunder of freedom.
> (*SR* 35)

If Crusz's version shows a genuine admiration for Sardiel, it also problematizes this figure, makes him human, while preserving the sense of magic that surrounds him. While the poem claims him as a freedom fighter, in another prose piece called the "Interview," when questioned by a reporter, Sardiel admits that his motives were not always so lofty:

> I am no freedom-fighter. My hatred for the Englishman was absolutely practical. If he suffered at my hands, and if his colonial image was bruised and bloodied, so be it, and let the lovers of freedom clap their hands.

The interview makes clear what is left unstated in "Bumpis"—notions of an exploitative society, of a clergy that was complicitous with the wealthy in its attitude to the poor, and the need to avenge the humiliation of being constantly ridiculed by the rich.

The more romantic notion of Sardiel is the subject of the bedtime story entitled "Katu Bawa and the Bandit" where the Robin Hood aspect is emphasized. Here the harshness is muted, and Sardiel is the saviour of the poor folk who are ruthlessly exploited by the merchants. In the prose pieces that follow, the image is made more complex and perspectives change.

Sardiel's childhood of deprivation, his love for the poor, his ruthlessness, his hatred for the Buddhist clergy, his conversion to Christianity at the end of his life, all these are documented in the various prose pieces. In the many stories associated with Sardiel, Crusz finds the opportunity to work with historical sources and transform them in a manner that demonstrates the fictiveness of legend and constructedness of history. For a writer who has, for the most part, avoided the use of history in his poems, the narrative of Sardiel allows for distance and a preoccupation with politics. And it is not far-fetched to claim that the issues which become the focus of this long narrative are similar to those that occupied the authors who dealt at length with the Insurgency of 1971.

"Sardiel" is about another time, another world. Not unlike "Bumpis," it accommodates the fantastic and the magical, and the historical significance of the retelling is not dependent on realism. It is, like the children's story, about survival, about class and power, about the justice meted out to the exploitative merchant, about the triumph of the underdog. The natural world evoked in the poetry is once again created here, in the natural setting of the Kadugannawa hills. The story is also the occasion for satire, particularly in the episode called "The Interview," in which the newspaper reporter with his middle-class sensibility, his naive morality, becomes the object of the blunt abuse of Sardiel. The story of Sardiel has remained more in the form of discontinuous narratives than as a complete work, and that is probably because what has been transformed into imaginative terms is still close to what has been recorded in historical accounts or retained as folk tale and legend. What one hopes for is that the fictive will merge with the "historical" to produce a larger work of prose that will serve as an integral part of the total work of the poet.

Equally important among the eclectic prose writings are a series of memoirs, numbered in sequence, all dedicated to his mother, Cleta Nora Marcellina Serpanchy, and called "Tough Love," "The Beachcomber," "Maria Takes Antoni on Safari," "The Case of the Floating Soothers," "Code of Silence" and "Beating 'the Monsoon Blues.'" In these episodic narratives about the childhood memories of the author, the mother remains a constant presence, and if the narratives are a tribute to the mother whose love and discipline steered the eight children, it is also a splendid evocation of the 1930s, the days at the beach, the heady excitement of the Big Match between St. Joseph's and St. Peter's, little moments of love masked in iron discipline. As in "Beating . . ." historical moments—in this case a famous murder trial —"place" these fragments against a referential "public," backdrop. While not all the episodes self-consciously establish the relation between the private and the public, the private does serve as a synecdoche for the public while retaining the specificity of a particular family. To read these fragments (which, incidentally, are reminiscent of Ondaatje's narrative mode in *Running in the Family*) is to capture the spaciousness of the era, of a country moving towards independence. The sheer lyrical beauty of the passages captures something of that period. In "The Beachcomber" Crusz writes:

> I am here like a summer prayer—me, the seducing sun, blue water, sand crabs and seaweed. Home is now here, six hours to noon. I cup the thick salt water in my palms, rinse my mouth, wash my face. My feet, I hold to the frothing foam as it visits the shore with the rhythm of a heartbeat. The sand crabs know me, seem to trust me. They venture out to play hide and seek, take me to their porches, front doors in the sand, then suddenly disappear.

The sensuous appeal of nature that characterizes his poetry is a result of having been a part of this world. And these episodes stand in ironic contrast to the viciousness and betrayal of "Sardiel" and the desolation of "Bumpis." Together they traverse a whole historical period, moving from the factual to the personal and the magical. What unites all the prose pieces is the sense of magic, whether it is the presence of the elephant, the holy oils that, for a time, protected the outlaw, or the sheer beauty of a life lived in harmony with nature. All three testify to the commitment of the author to the country he left, and place him more securely among those diasporic writers for whom the fragments of the past are never really eclipsed.

How much for the earth, for a kilo of bread,
for the windfall of grapes, for the shoes on our feet.
How much mister, how much does it take ...

"Party's End"— PABLO NERUDA[1]

VI. WALKING IN THE PENUMBRA

In Book Six of Walcott's spectacular epic about the Caribbean, *Omeros*, the author finds the occasion to meditate on the poet's craft, his own complicity in the colonisation of his people. He wonders:

> . . . didn't I want the poor
> to stay in the same light so that I could transfix
> them in amber, the afterglow of empire,[2]

and a few lines later, asks more specifically, "Hadn't I made their poverty my paradise?" Here one finds the ongoing dilemma of the diasporic poet, the nagging self-doubt about the vocation, the need to interrogate the discursive field within which one operates. The dividing line between a spokesperson and a "native informant" (to borrow Gayatri Spivak's term) is often thin and poets who write in English and who count among their audience predominantly a Western readership are particularly prone to one or the other. And this is exactly what Walcott sees as Naipaul's project in *Enigma of Arrival*, and in a polemical review of the novel castigates the novel for achieving his success at an obscene cost.[3]

Very much along the same lines Aijaz Ahmad discusses Rushdie's treatment of Pakistan in *Shame*. According to Ahmad, Rushdie transforms the sense of loss, the void associated with exile into "excess" as he locates himself on the cusp of East and West and orientalises the former in order to find acceptance in the latter.[4] Whether the charge against Rushdie is true or not, what the analysis makes abundantly clear is that the old model of exile as loss, an argument advanced by William Walsh and others like him, is hardly valid for immigrant writers today.

The intellectual basis of Robert Crusz's film *In Between* is none other than this ongoing quest. Although the title implies the stasis of hybridity—the middle ground—the more insistent concern is with quest, with a definition of self that will merge the private and the public without an exoticism that masquerades as sincere nostalgia. The film celebrates the past but refuses to seek fixity in the present. What Robert Crusz sees in his uncle Rienzi Crusz's poetry is what he asserts at the end of his film: a constant movement. In that ambivalence one sees an echo of the sentiments of Michael Ondaatje in *Running in the Family* where the author defines his role in careful terms:

> During certain hours, at certain years in our lives, we see ourselves as remnants from the earlier generations that were destroyed. So our job becomes to keep peace with the enemy camps, eliminate the chaos at the end of Jacobean tragedies, and "with the mercy of distance" write the histories.[5]

For Rienzi Crusz too the notion of home has become a multilayered concept, a shifting one depending on the stance he adopts. At both ends of the spectrum are the referential; on the one hand, the quotidian realities of Canada as expressed in "Summertime at Waterloo Park," and on the other the landscapes of Sri Lanka as described in "Michael." If, in a general sense, irony characterises the "Canadian" poems and nostalgia underscores the Sri Lankan ones, such dichotomies express, at best, provisional truths. The consciousness of the immigrant hardly ever settles into such comfortable binaries, and Crusz's poetry is again a refusal to take such totalizing positions. Both Canada and Sri Lanka are seen anew as the poet moves from one to the other, celebrating, castigating and ironizing.

These two ends are the more "multicultural" aspects of Crusz and link him with a large number of writers Asian, African, and European, who make the intersection of two or more cultures their subject. In these poems, Crusz is very much the hyphenated poet, mediating multiple worlds, offering "Splitting Images." In these he is a poet with a mission, with a commitment to expose antipathy that masquerades as tolerance and compassion.

Between these two lies another world—in the light and shade of a penumbra—where the personal and the abstract meet. This is where the poet gives expression to a private world, one that is framed by an equally private mythology. Despite the conventional elements that establish a distance between the author and his work, intentionality persists, and the poems invite the reader to eavesdrop on the experience of the poet. And the emotion generated by the personal is kept in check by an elaborate system of mythology that invokes the world of animals, fruits and nature of Sri Lanka. And it is not in the finely wrought minimalist poems but in the emotionally charged exuberant works that Crusz's distinctive voice is to be heard.

This world is both ambivalent and paradoxical. On the one hand, the voice is Canadian in its understanding of the nation but is expressed through a sensibility that is distinctly Sri Lankan. The language system is Sri Lankan, in its registers, its phrases, its use of proper nouns, but the poetic mode is clearly western. The stanzaic patterns are Western while the weltanschauung is Sri Lankan. And if his poetry captures something of the spontaneity and artlessness of much contemporary writing, it also contains that sense of conscious choice. The rhythms of speech merge seamlessly with a poetic voice. This is a grey area within which he functions and one in which he found his distinctive voice.

On the last day of 1996, Crusz wrote a poem entitled "Homecomings" which, appropriately, through the metaphors of river and sea asserts a sense of closure. The sea as mother and the river as prodigal child reinforce finality. But the most memorable lines of the poem are about the meandering path of the river which, as it touches and transforms—and is transformed—by everything it encounters, changes the focus to movement rather than closure. And by the same token, whether he chooses to visit Sri Lanka or remain in Canada, he is equally at home, but always with a certainty that neither one is unequivocally home. As the last stanza puts it:

> I've meandered
> this way and that,
> from shore to shore, one love
> to another, blue skies to cumulus cloud—
> under an umbrella of doting children,
> still going unafraid laughing,
> the blood fevering like some mischievous child—
> always knowing the beginning,
> the journey's throbbing walk
> to this igloo of heaven

or that sun-faced island of the elephant
where I'm always at home,
if not home.

In the passionate exploration of these multiple realities Crusz's poetry stands apart from many other writers. Successful or not, this is what his contribution is likely to be. Critics have found in his work a striking resemblance to the poetry of Dylan Thomas and Pablo Neruda. While the intersections in subject matter that link the three poets is in itself interesting, the more significant connection lies in the voice of passion. Whether Crusz portrays the defiance of a rebellious priest or describes the dance of restless ghosts in a cemetery, a sense of heightened emotion pervades the poems. Even when the poet contemplates his old age in the poem "Libra," the language transcends the solemnity of the subject to express a cosmic vision made possible by a faith in the redemptive power of passion:

No. I will not "go gently into that dark night"
You'll first hear
the Kandyan drums make fire
under the dancer's anklet bells,
the raven caw the breaking news,
the elephant's last clear trumpet—
and I, wearing the skullcap
of the noonday sun, rosary in hand,
will seek the kingdom of God,
with the face of a sinner,
and the soul of a faltering saint.

Perhaps a fitting conclusion to this study could be the words of Irving Layton who, in a letter to Crusz dated 2 March 1972, wrote: "I can't think of a single poet who, groin tickled and happy, could achieve such delirium on paper."[6]

NOTES

1. WRITING AGAINST THE GRAIN

1. *A Memory of Asia* (Austin, Texas: Curbstone Publishing, 1984), 29.

2 "The Last Expatriate," in *The Oxford Anthology of Australian Literature*, eds. Leonie Kramer and Adrian Mitchell (Melbourne: Oxford University Press, 1985), 335.

3. Ibid., 333.

4. Ibid., 336.

5. See *The Predicament of Culture: Twentieth Century Ethnography, Literature, Art* (Cambridge, Mass.: Harvard University Press, 1988), 1-17, and *Imaginary Homelands* (London: Granta, 1991), 9-21.

6. *Patrick White Speaks* (London: Jonathan Cape, 1990), 15.

7. Ibid., 14.

8. Ibid., 17.

9 Aamer Hussein, "The Echoing of Quiet Voices," in *Asian Voices in English*, eds. Mimi Chan and Roy Harris (Hong Kong: Hong Kong University Press, 1991), 102.

10 See *Imaginary Homelands*, 12.

11. Vijay Mishra, "The Diasporic Imaginary: Theorizing the Indian Diaspora," *Textual Practice* 10, no. 3 (1996): 433-34.

12. See *Borderlands/La Frontera: The New Mestiza* (San Francisco: Aunt Lute Books, 1987), 79.

13. Mishra, 421. Says Mishra: "This narrative of diasporic movement is, however, not continuous or seamless as there is a radical break between the older diasporas of classic capitalism and the mid- to late twentieth-century diasporas of advanced capital to the metropolitan centres of the Empire, the New World and the former settler colonies."

14. Aijaz Ahmad, *In Theory: Classes, Nations, Literatures* (London: Verso, 1992), 127. According to Ahmad, "this myth of ontological unbelonging is replaced by another, larger myth of *excess* of belongings: not that he belongs nowhere, but that he belongs to *too many* places."

15. See "Night Rain on the Parapet," *The Guardian*, 17 May 1990, p. 21.

16. "Caliban," in *Testimonies of Exile* (Trenton, New Jersey: Africa World Press, 1990), 5.

17. See "But you like what you see," in *Becaue of India* (London: Onlywomen Press, 1989), 118.

18. Linda Hutcheon, *Splitting Images: Contemporary Canadian Ironies* (Toronto: Oxford University Press, 1991), 64.

19. Rienzi Crusz, letter regarding organizing a poetry presentation at Lakehead University, Thunder Bay, 19-22 October 1983.

20. Letter to Rienzi Crusz, 16 March 1993.

21. Letter to Rienzi Crusz, 6 April 1973.

22. Letter to Rienzi Crusz, 1 July 1985.

23. Craig Tapping, "Front Lines," *Canadian Literature* 117 (Summer 1988): 147.

24. Suwanda H J Sugunasiri, " 'Sri Lankan' Canadian Poets: The Bourgeoisie That Fled the Revolution," *Canadian Literature* 132 (Spring 1992): 67.

25. "Talking for Myself," *The Toronto South Asian Review* 6 (Summer 1987): 35.

26. Letter to Rienzi Crusz, 8 May 1974.

27. Letter to Rienzi Crusz, 27 August 1986.

28. W K Thomas, review of *Flesh and Thorn*, *Gazette*, 19 June 1974.

29. M Thorpe, review of *The Rain Doesn't Know Me Any More*, *World Literature Today* 68 (1994): 130.

30. Robert Crusz, " 'Weathervane Meanings' and the Fourth World Poet: Identity As Liberation in the Poetry of Rienzi Crusz," (unpublished), 3.

31. Hutcheon, *Splitting Images*, 151.

32. The term "Burgher" refers to people of mixed Eurasian ancestry, who are generally identified by the lightness of their complexion, their use of English as their mother tongue and their Westernization. It is also a general belief that Dutch Burghers tend to be fairer than Portuguese Burghers.

33. See *Other Solitudes: Canadian Multicultural Fictions*, eds. Linda Hutcheon and Marion Richmond (Toronto: Oxford University Press, 1990), 202.

34. Arun Mukherjee, "Two Responses to Otherness: The Poetry of Michael Ondaatje and Cyril Dabydeen," *Journal of Commonwealth Literature* 20, no. 1 (1985): 49-67.

35. Arun Mukherjee, "Songs of an Immigrant: The Poetry of Rienzi Crusz," *Currents* 4, no. 1 (1986/87): 21.

36. Ranu Samantrai, "States of Belonging: Pluralism, Migrancy, Literature," *Essays on Canadian Writing* 57 (Winter 1995): 47.

37. See *Unending Design: The Forms of Postmodern Poetry* (Ithaca and London: Cornell University Press, 1991).

38. Thorpe, 130.

38. An unpublished children's story written in Sri Lanka.

39. Uma Parameswaran, "The Singing Metaphor: Poetry of Rienzi Crusz," *Canadian Literature* 132 (Spring 1992): 147.

40. Robert Crusz, 8.

2. CHILD OF A COLONIAL EMBRACE

1. *The Star-Apple Kingdom* (London: Jonathan Cape, 1980), 4.
2. Unpublished.
3. Uma Parameswaran, "The Singing Metaphor," 146. Along similar lines, Judith Miller says that Crusz's poems "carry a language of modulated rhythm and sonority, the language of oral poetry and of the King James version of the Bible." See "Archangel and Charlie's Angel: The Poetry of Rienzi Crusz," *The Toronto South Asian Review* 10, no. 2 (1992): 66.
4. Noel Crusz, "A Don's Journey to Science and God," *Catholic Messenger*, 2 July 1983, p. 9.
5. Letter to Chelva Kanaganayakam, 7 January 1996.
6. Noel Crusz, 9.
7. *In Between*, Sankofa Films and Video, 1992.
8. "Talking for Myself," 32.
9. *Running in the Family*, 32.
10. Letter to Rienzi Crusz, 13 February, 1991.
11. "Exile," in *Trial by Terror* (Hamilton, NZ: Rimu, 1987), 14.
12. "Talking," 32.
13. Ibid., 33.
14. "The Singing Metaphor," 149.
15. Unpublished poem.
16. "Talking," 30.
17. Ibid., 31.
18. Derek Walcott, "Mass Man" in *Collected Poems 1948-84* (New York: Farrar, Straus & Giroux, 1986), 99.
19. Letter to Rienzi Crusz, 13 February, 1991.
20. "The End of Poetry," *Canadian Literature* 115 (Winter 1987): 130.
21. *Making it Real: The Canonization of English-Canadian Literature* (Concord, Ontario: Anansi, 1995), 130.
22. Ahmed, *In Theory*, 123.
23. "Papayas and Red River Cereal," *Canadian Literature* 132 (Spring 1992): 3.
24. Ibid., 6.
25. *Canadian Voices* (Delhi: Pencraft, 1996), 3.

3. PADDY FIELDS AND SNOW PLOUGHS

1. *Selected Poems: 1940-1989* (London: Penguin, 1990), 89.
2. "Songs of an Immigrant," 21.
3. *Canadian Voices*, 10.

4. Letter to Rienzi Crusz, 18 June 1974.

5. Letter to Rienzi Crusz, 6 March 1969.

6. "Dark Eruptions, Muted Ways," review of *Flesh and Thorn*, *The Globe and Mail*, 24 August 1974.

7. Review of *Flesh and Thorn*, *Applegarth's Folly*, 2 (1975): 8.

8. "Talking," 19.

9. "Songs of an Immigrant," 19.

10. "Exoticism and Ethnicity in Michael Ondaatje's *Running in the Family*," *Essays on Canadian Writing*," 57 (1995): 116.

11. *Closed Entrances* (Toronto: TSAR, 1994) and *Selling Illusions: The Cult of Multiculturalism in Canada* (Toronto: Penguin, 1994).

12. "Songs of an Immigrant," 19.

13. Ibid., 19.

14. Huggan, 123.

15. Miller, 76.

16. See *Literature in English*, eds. W H New and W E Messenger (Scarborough, Ontario: Prentice-Hall, 1993), 1491-92.

17. See Arnold H Itwaru, *Body Rites* (Toronto: TSAR, 1991), 27.

18. See David Dabydeen, *Coolie Odyssey* (London: Hansib/Dangaroo, 1988), 17.

19. Letter to Rienzi Crusz, 23 May 1971.

20. "How Hyphenated Can You Get?: A Critique of Pure Ethnicity," *Mosaic* 29, no. 3 (1996): 113.

21. Letter to Rienzi Crusz, 10 November 1982.

22. Huggan, 117.

23. Tapping, 147.

24. Sugunasiri, 65.

25. See Noel Crusz, "A Don's Journey . . ."

26. "Talking," 33.

27. "Rienzi Crusz," in *Writers of the Indian Diaspora: A Bio- Bibliographical Critical Sourcebook*, ed. Emmanuel S Nelson (Westport, Connecticut: Greenwood Press, 1993), 60.

28. Letter to Rienzi Crusz, 8 April, 1990.

29. *World Literature Today*, 68 (1994), 130.

30. "The Sri Lankan Poets in Canada: An Alternative View," *The Toronto South Asian Review* 3, no. 2 (1984): 39.

31. Letter to Rienzi Crusz, 28 Sept. 1989.

4. A DEATH SO EXOTICALLY DONE

1. See "Sunday Morning," in *20th Century Poetry and Poetics*, ed. Gary

Geddes (Toronto: Oxford, 1973), 117.

2. Says Layton: "I envy you the girl and the poems they inspired. Why doesn't someone with 'torches in (her) limbs' come my way? I'd put them out with the most sublime and magnificent ejaculations, and I'd keep on doing so at the slightest hint of flame or fire." See Francis Mansbridge, ed. *Wild Gooseberries: The Selected Letters of Irving Layton* (Toronto: Macmillan, 1989), 274-75.

3. See "Weathervane Meanings."

4. In a letter dated 15 August 1996, Ghose mentions that such lines "sound like philosophical posturing."

5. See *Poetic Artifice: A Theory of Twentieth-Century Poetry* (Manchester: Manchester University Press, 1978).

6. Forrest-Thomson, 59.

7. *The Rhetoric of the Contemporary Lyric* (Bloomington: Indiana University Press, 1980), 18.

8. *Come Back to Me My Language: Poetry and the West Indies* (Toronto: McClelland and Stewart, 1993), 197.

9. See *A Memory of Asia*, 3-6.

10. Review of *Beatitudes of Ice*, *World Literature Today* 70 (1996): 696. According to Thorpe, "Crusz's free but carefully constructed verse should be read aloud to capture its movement, althought its rhythms are best heard in the poet's rich tones—which, ideally, one would like to hear packaged in an accompanying CD."

11. Along similar lines, Andrew Stubbs in a very perceptive essay states: "But placing too much stress on such stable features can compel the critic to become fixated on the outward or, perhaps, paraphrasable content of Crusz's work, which would be to ignore another crucial factor: its performative aspect, its sensuous dimension, its physical immediacy and intimacy." See "Keeping Iago: Rituals of Innocence in Rienzi Crusz's Recent Poetry" (unpublished).

12. See *Lyric Poetry: Beyond New Criticism* (Ithaca and London: Cornell University Press, 1985), 31. Says Frye: "The more this sense of the discontinuous increases, the more closely we approach the lyrical area."

5. VISIONS, CONFESSIONS AND MEMOIRS

1. See *The Arrivants: A New World Trilogy* (Oxford: OxfordUniversity Press, 1981), 122.

2. *Children's Literature in Canada* (New York: Twayne, 1992), 7.

3. Ibid., 6.

6. WALKING IN THE PENUMBRA

1. *Pablo Neruda: A New Decade (Poems 1958-1967)*, ed. Ben Belitt (New York: Grove Press, 1969), 121.

2. New York: Farrar, Straus & Giroux, 1990, p. 227.

3. "The Garden Path," review of *The Enigma of Arrival*, by V S Naipaul, *The New Republic*, 13 April 1987, pp. 27-31. Walcott writes: "If the world that Naipaul left behind for others to care about has, for the descendents of slave and indentured worker, neither Art nor Culture, neither flower gardens nor venerable elms, it is because none of that was given to the slave or the indentured worker. To write about this lack as if it were the fault of the African and the Indian is not only to betray them, but to lie" (30).

4. *In Theory*, 127.

5. *Running in the Family*, 179.

6. Letter to Rienzi Crusz.

SELECTED BIBLIOGRAPHY

PART 1

A. Works by Rienzi Crusz

Poetry Collections

Flesh and Thorn. Stratford, Ont.: Pasdeloup Press, 1974.
Elephant and Ice. Erin, Ont.: Porcupine's Quill, 1980.
Singing Against the Wind. Erin, Ont.: Porcupine's Quill, 1985.
A Time for Loving. Toronto: TSAR, 1986.
Still Close to the Raven. Toronto: TSAR, 1989.
The Rain Doesn't Know Me Any More. Toronto: TSAR, 1992.
Beatitudes of Ice. Toronto: TSAR, 1995.

Essays

"Talking for Myself." *The Toronto South Asian Review* 6, no. 1 (1987): 29-35.

Unpublished Works

"Bumpis, the Magic Elephant." Children's story.
"Sardiel." Narrative of prose and poetry.
"And Then There Was One." Poem.
"Sardiel Runs the Blockade." Poem.
"By Reason of Black Magic." Prose.
"A Bodyguard for Mr Silva." Prose.
"The Dowry." Poem.
"Katu Bawa and the Bandit." Prose.
"The Word Made Flesh." Poem.
"Note to Mammaley Marikar." Prose.
"Sardiel Is Coming. Sardiel Is Coming." Prose.
"Judas." Poem.
"The Gospel According to Sardiel." Prose.
"Interview." Prose.
"Legends of Fear." Poem.

Dark Antonyms and Paradise

Recollections and fictions dedicated to Cleta Nora Marcellina Serpanchy consisting of the following works:

"Tough Love."
"The Beachcomber."
"Maria Takes Antoni on Safari."
"The Case of the Floating Soothers."
"Code of Silence."
"Beating the 'Monsoon Blues'."

Letters

Regarding the organization of a poetry presentation at Lakehead University, Thunder Bay. 19 October 1983.

To Chelva Kanaganayakam. 7 January 1996.

B. Criticism on the Works of Rienzi Crusz

Articles

Crusz, Noel. "A Don's Journey to Science and God." *Catholic Messenger*, 2 July 1983.

Crusz, Robert. " 'Weathervane Meanings' and the Fourth World Poet: Identity As Liberation in the Poetry of Rienzi Crusz." Photocopy.

Miller, Judith. "Archangel and Charlie's Angel: The Poems of Rienzi Crusz." *The Toronto South Asian Review* 10, no. 2 (1992): 66-76.

Mukherjee, Arun. "Songs of an Immigrant: The Poetry of Rienzi Crusz." *Currents: Readings in Race Relations* 4, no. 1 (1986/87): 19-21.

———. "The Sri Lankan Poets in Canada: An Alternative View." *The Toronto South Asian Review* 3, no. 2 (1984): 32-45.

Parameswaran, Uma. "The Singing Metaphor: Poetry of Rienzi Crusz." *Canadian Literature* 132 (Spring 1992): 145-54.

———. "Rienzi Crusz." In *Writers of the Indian Diaspora: A Bio-Bibliographical Critical Sourcebook*. Edited by Emmanuel S Nelson. Westport, Connecticut: Greenwood Press, 1993.

Stubbs, Andrew. "Keeping Iago: Rituals of Innocence in Rienzi Crusz's Recent Poetry." Photocopy.

Sugunasiri, Suwanda J. " 'Sri Lankan' Canadian Poets: The Bourgeoisie That Fled the Revolution." *Canadian Literature* 132 (Spring 1992): 60-79.

Films

Crusz, Robert. *In Between.* Sankofa Films and Video, 1992.

Reviews

Barnes, W J. Review of *Flesh and Thorn. Quarry* (Winter 1975): 79-80.

Kanaganayakam, Chelva. Review of *Beatitudes of Ice,* by Rienzi Crusz and *The Faces of Galle Face Green* by Suwanda Sugunasiri. *The Toronto Review of Contemporary Writing Abroad* 14, no. 3 (1996): 78-81.

McKay, Don. Review of *Flesh and Thorn. Applegarth's Folly* 2 (1975): 18-19.

Parameswaran, Uma. Review of *Still Close to the Raven. World Literature Today* 65 (Winter 1991): 116-17.

Selvadurai, Shyam. Review of *Beatitudes of Ice. Books in Canada* 25, no. 5 (1996): 25.

Stevens, Peter. Review of *Flesh and Thorn. The Globe and Mail* 24 August 1974.

Tapping, Craig. "Front Lines." Review of *Echosmos* by Hedi Bouraoui, *A Time for Loving* by Rienzi Crusz, *Letters from the Equator* by C H Gervais. *Canadian Literature* 117 (Summer 1988): 145-47.

Thorpe, Michael. Review of *The Rain Doesn't Know Me Any More. World Literature Today* 68 (1994): 130.

———. Review of *Beatitudes of Ice. World Literature Today* 70 (1996): 696.

Correspondence

Ahearn, Catherine. Letter to Rienzi Crusz. 23 May 1971.

Atwood, Margaret. Letter to Rienzi Crusz. 23 May 1971.

Birney, Earle. Letter to Rienzi Crusz. 6 April 1973.

Crusz, Hilary. Letter to Rienzi Crusz. 18 June 1974.

Ghose, Zulfikar. Letter to Rienzi Crusz. 15 August 96.

Gutteridge, Don. Letter to Rienzi Crusz. 16 March 1993.

Itwaru, Arnold. Letter to Rienzi Crusz. 28 September 1989.

Lane, Travis. Letter to Rienzi Crusz. 13 February 1991.

Layton, Irving. Letter to Rienzi Crusz. 6 March 1969.

PART 2

Works Cited

Ahmad, Aijaz. *In Theory: Classes, Nations, Literature*. London: Verso, 1992.

Anzaldúa, Gloria. *Borderlands/La Frontera: The New Mestiza*. San Francisco: Aunt Lute Books, 1987.

Arasanayagam, Jean. *Trial by Terror*. Hamilton, NZ: Rimu, 1987.

Belitt, Ben, editor. *Pablo Neruda: A New Decade (Poems 1958-1967)*. New York: Grove Press, 1969.

Bissoondath, Neil. *Selling Illusions: The Cult of Multiculturalism in Canada*. Toronto: Penguin, 1994.

Brathwaite, Edward. *The Arrivants: A New World Trilogy*. 1973. Reprint, Oxford: Oxford University Press, 1981.

Busia, Abena. *Testimonies of Exile*. Trenton, New Jersey: Africa World Press, 1990.

Chamberlin, Edward J. *Come Back to Me My Language*. Toronto: McClelland and Stewart, 1993.

Clifford, James. *The Predicament of Culture: Twentieth-Century Ethnography, Literature, and Art*. Cambridge, Mass.: Harvard University Press, 1988.

Conte, Joseph M. *Unending Design: The Forms of Postmodern Poetry*. Ithaca and London: Cornell University Press, 1991.

Dabydeen, David. *Coolie Odyssey*. London: Hansib/Dangaroo, 1988.

Forrest-Thomson, Veronica. *Poetic Artifice: A Theory of Twentieth-Century Poetry*. Manchester: Manchester University Press, 1978.

Frye, Northrop. "Approaching the Lyric." In *Lyric Poetry: Beyond New Criticism*. Edited by Chaviva Hosek and Patricia Parker. Ithaca and London: Cornell University Press, 1985.

Ghose, Zulfikar. *A Memory of Asia*. Austin, Texas: Curbstone Press, 1984.

Heath, Roy. "Night Rain on the Parapet." *The Guardian*, 17 May 1990.

Holden, Jonathan. *The Rhetoric of the Contemporary Lyric*. Bloomington: Indiana University Press, 1980.

Huggan, Graham. "Exoticism and Ethnicity in Michael Ondaatje's *Running in the Family*." *Essays on Canadian Writing* 57 (Winter 1995): 116-127.

Hussein, Aamer. "The Echoing of Quiet Voices." In *Asian Voices in English*. Edited by Mimi Chan and Roy Harris. Hong Kong: Hong Kong University Press, 1991.

Hutcheon, Linda. *Splitting Images: Contemporary Canadian Ironies*. Toronto: Oxford University Press, 1991.

Hutcheon, Linda and Marion Richmond, editors. *Other Solitudes: Canadian*

Multicultural Fictions. Oxford: Oxford University Press, 1990.

Itwaru, Arnold Harrichand. *Closed Entrances: Canadian Culture and Imperialism*. Toronto: TSAR, 1994.

———. "Arrival." In *Body Rites*. Toronto: TSAR, 1994.

Kershaw, Alister. "The Last Expatriate." In *The Oxford Anthology of Australian Literature*. Edited by Leonie Kramer and Adrian Mitchell. Melbourne: Oxford University Press, 1985.

Kudchedkar, Shirin and Jameela Begum, editors. *Canadian Voices*. Delhi: Pencraft International, 1996.

Lecker, Robert. *Making it Real: The Canonization of English-Canadian Literature*. Concord, Ontario: Anansi, 1995.

Mansbridge, Francis, editor. *Wild Gooseberries: The Selected Letters of Irving Layton*. Toronto: Macmillan, 1990.

Mishra, Vijay. "The Diasporic Imaginary: Theorizing the Indian Diaspora." *Textual Practice* 10 (1996): 421-447.

Mukherjee, Arun. "Two Responses to Otherness: The Poetry of Michael Ondaatje and Cyril Dabydeen." *Journal of Commonwealth Literature* 20, no. 1 (1985): 49-67.

Namjoshi, Suniti. *Because of India*. London: Onlywomen Press, 1989.

New, W H. "Papayas and Red River Cereal." *Canadian Literature* 132 (Spring 1992): 3-6.

New, WH and W E Messenger, editors. *Literature in English*. Scarborough, Ont.: Prentice-Hall, 1993.

Ondaatje, Michael. *Running in The Family*. Toronto: McClelland and Stewart, 1982.

Rushdie, Salman. *Imaginary Homelands*. London: Granta, 1991.

Samantrai, Ranu. "States of Belonging: Pluralism, Migrancy, Literature." *Essays on Canadian Writing* 57 (Winter 1995): 33-50.

Solway, David. "The End of Poetry." *Canadian Literature* 115 (Winter 1987): 127-134.

Soyinka, Wole. "Telephone Conversation." In *Literature in English*. Edited by W H New and W E Messenger. Scarborough, Ont.: Prentice-Hall, 1993.

Stevens, Wallace. "Sunday Morning." In *20th Century Poetry and Poetics*. Ed. Gary Geddes. Toronto: Oxford University Press, 1973.

Verhoven, W M. "How Hyphenated Can you Get? A Critique of Pure Ethnicity." *Mosaic* 29 (1996): 97-116.

Walcott, Derek. *The Star-Apple Kingdom*. London: Jonathan Cape, 1980.

———. *Omeros*. New York: Farrar, Straus & Giroux, 1990.

———. *Collected Poems 1948-1984*. New York: Farrar, Straus & Giroux, 1986.

———. "The Garden Path." Review of *The Enigma of Arrival*, by V S Naipaul. *The New Republic* 13 April 1987: 27-31.

Waterston, Elizabeth. *Children's Literature in Canada*. New York: Twayne, 1992.

White, Patrick. "The Prodigal Son." In *Patrick White Speaks*. (London: Jonathan Cape, 1990).

Wijesinha, Rajiva, editor. *An Anthology of Contemporary Sri Lankan Poetry in English*. 1988. Reprint, Colombo: The English Association of Sri Lanka, n.d.

INDEX

Ahmad, Aijaz, 4, 28, 69, 73 n. 14
American Poet, 25
Anzaldúa, Gloria, 3
Arasanayagam, Jean, 22
Atwood, Margaret, 13, 36
Bhabha, Homi, 10
Bhakti literature, 49
Birney, Earle, 7, 27
Bissoondath, Neil, 33
Blake, William, 45, 50
Bloom, Harold, 10
Bly, Robert, 27
Brathwaite, Edward, 58, 62
Buddhism, 51
Burghers, 12, 18, 20, 21, 22, 43, 64, 74 n. 32
Burnett, Virgil, 27
Busia, Abena, 4, 5
Canada, 5, 6, 9, 14, 71
Canadian Literature, 7, 28
Canadian Forum, 15, 25, 31
Canadian Voices, 29
Cardinal Poetry Quarterly, 25
Castle Hill, 2
Catholicism, 16, 48
Chamberlin, J E, 53
Chevron, 25
Clifford, James, 2, 73 n. 5
Conte, Joseph, 14
Crusz, Hilary, 18, 19, 20, 23, 31, 48
Crusz, Michael, 18-19
Crusz, Robert, 10, 16, 49, 60, 74 n. 30
  In Between, 20, 69-70
Crusz, Noel, 19, 20, 39, 48
Curnow, Allen, 30
Dabydeen, Cyril, 12, 33, 36
Descant, 25
Dust, A I, 9
Eliot, T S, 26
Emecheta, Buchi, 10
Fiddlehead, 15, 31
Forrest-Thomson, Veronica, 52, 58
Frye, Northrop, 60, 78 n. 12
Ghose, Zulfikar, 1, 6, 9, 27, 42, 51, 53, 57, 77 n. 4
Gool, Reshard, 7, 45
Grail, 49
Gutteridge, Don, 7
Harris, Wilson, 10
Harwood, Harold, 27
Heath, Roy, 4
Hinduism, 16, 49, 51
Holden, Jonathan, 52, 53
Hussein, Aamer, 3
Hutcheon, Linda, 11
Itwaru, Arnold, 33, 36, 44
Keats, John, 54,55
Keneally, Thomas, 10
Kershaw, Alister, 1-2, 3, 5
Lane, Travis, 6, 22, 27
Larkin, Philip, 52
Layton, Irving, 6, 7, 13, 27, 31, 46, 72, 77 n. 2
Liontayles, 25
Malahat Review, 15
Miller, Judith, 75 n. 3
Mishra, Vijay, 3, 4, 73 n. 13
Mistry, Rohinton, 4
Moore, Marianne, 27
Mukherjee, Arun, 12, 13, 26, 27, 30, 32, 44
Naipaul, V S, 8
Namjoshi, Suniti, 4, 5
"Native Informant," 69
Neruda, Pablo, 21, 25, 69, 72
New, W H, 29
New York Quarterly, 25
Okigbo, Christopher, 50-51

Ondaatje, Michael, 4, 8, 12, 16, 18, 27, 44, 59
Running in the Family, 18, 22, 24, 27, 33, 67, 70
Parameswaran, Uma, 13, 15, 18, 23, 27, 35, 42
Peter Pan, 63
Portuguese, 18
Prairie Schooner, 15
Prism International, 25
Richards, I A., 20
Romanticism, 14, 16, 46, 60
Rushdie, Salman, 2, 3, 4, 69, 73 n. 5
Samantrai, Ranu, 13
Sardiel, 24, 42, 65-67
Sinhalese, 8, 18, 64
Soyinka, Wole, 14, 36
Sri Lanka, 5, 6, 8, 10, 11, 12, 14, 15, 24, 41, 61, 71
Stevens, Wallace, 45
Stubbs, Andrew, 78 n. 11
Sugunasiri, Suwanda, 8, 39
Tamils, 18
Tapping, Craig, 7, 8, 15, 38-39, 43
Thomas, Dylan, 23, 26, 72
Thomas, W K, 9
Thompson, Francis, 19
Thorpe, Michael, 9, 13, 14, 27, 44, 56, 78 n. 10
Toronto South Asian Review, 27
United Poets, 25
Vassanji, M G, 28
Voices International, 25
Walcott, Derek, 10, 14, 17, 26, 29, 40
Omeros, 29, 69
White, Patrick, 2, 5
"The Prodigal Son," 2
Whitman, Walt, 26, 56
Wijesinha, Rajiva, 12
Wizard of Oz, 63
Yeats, W B, 47